P9-BVH-914

The HORSE

The HORSE

Passion · Beauty · Splendor · Strength

Elaine Walker

Parragon

Bath · New York · Cologne · Melbourne · Delhi
Hong Kong · Shenzhen · Singapore · Amsterdam

This edition published by Parragon Books Ltd and
distributed by

Parragon Inc.
440 Park Avenue South, 13th Floor
New York, NY 10016
www.parragon.com

Copyright © Parragon Books Ltd 2014

Text by Elaine Walker
Edited by Philip de Ste. Croix
Designed by Sue Pressley
Produced and packaged by Stonecastle Graphics Ltd
Project managed by Andrea O'Connor
Production by Joe Xavier

All rights reserved. No part of this publication
may be reproduced, stored in a retrieval system, or
transmitted, in any form or by any means, electronic,
mechanical, photocopying, recording, or otherwise,
without the prior permission of the copyright holder.

ISBN 978-1-4723-5146-3

Printed in China

Front cover © Getty Images/Anett Somogyvari

Dedicated to Rowan and Ruby

Author acknowledgements:
The author would like to thank Jennifer Sheerin
of Western Tack Trader, Ross Delap of Roslay
Shetland Ponies, and Louise Parker of Trevor
Hall Farm Curly Horses for help with research.
Special thanks as always to Alison Layland and
Martine Bailey as first readers of the text.

Contents

Introduction

Elaine Walker

The horse is an animal that has inspired humans in countless ways for at least 4,000 years. Images of horses are found both in the oldest known wall paintings and in today's most contemporary art. In the history of world civilization, the horse has often been the crucial factor that has facilitated travel, exploration, and growth. Empires have been founded, established, expanded, and even ultimately lost on horseback. In today's culture, the horse is primarily linked to leisure activities, and it remains one of the most popular and familiar animals, found living alongside people across the world in a fascinating variety of shapes, sizes, and colors.

Left to themselves, horses generally choose a quiet life, wandering in search of the best grazing and spending long periods of time just loafing around in herd groups. While they are born ready to run away from danger at high speed, they usually move in a relaxed way, instinctively conserving their energy. Yet they have carried humans over millions of miles, worked in farms, communities, and businesses, and frequently gone into battle. None of these activities are natural to the horse, yet the potential for willing companionship is at the heart of this most successful of partnerships.

This book is filled with wonderful images of horses embodying the spirit and beauty that make them so visually attractive to us. It also looks at the reasons why a horse will carry or follow a trusted human anywhere, even into situations that all its natural instincts tell it to avoid. Once we understand this, the spirit of the horse opens up to us and we can see more clearly how privileged we are to enjoy an enduring bond with this beautiful and sensitive animal.

I have kept horses all my life and watching them live as a herd is an ongoing lesson in instinct and body language. Recently, my own small herd of four Appaloosa horses and two donkeys have been sharing their fields with a herd of six Miniature Shetland ponies. It has been fascinating to watch the groups interact. They got to know one another over a fence and, by the time I let them all in together, they were already friendly. The tiny ponies mixed in straight away with my much larger horses, who are all 15 to 16 hands high. But the identity of the two groups has remained constant, even while they mingle and wander around the fields together. Often I'll look out of the window and see them a field apart, two entirely distinct groups, yet an hour later they will be gathered together in one large group. The donkeys usually do entirely their own thing and may or may not be with the horses, but they are always together.

Within the miniature pony herd there are several youngsters, aged from one to three years old. They have bonded with my two-year-old Appaloosa-Quarter Horse filly, Ruby, and she frequently wanders around in the middle of a knee-high entourage, so creating a third group of young horses made up of individuals from the two established herds. It is noticeable that while the boldest young Shetland will leave her herd completely and join my horses, Ruby only joins the Shetland group when they are fairly close to her own herd.

There is also a matriarch among the Shetlands, and I've watched my 15-hand baby being disciplined by this diminutive mare more than once. She does nothing but swing her head when she does not want Ruby to pass her and Ruby stands, waiting for permission to move. So far as I can tell, there is no reason for this other than to remind Ruby to be polite. In my own herd of two elderly geldings and another young mare, Ruby is allowed a certain amount of leeway, so perhaps to this tiny older horse things have got just a bit too relaxed!

This sort of fascinating observation is available to anyone with time to stand and watch a group of horses in a field. Sometimes it is an advantage not to know the horses because initial impressions will not be based on familiarity with individual characters.

This book allows me to share with you some of the pleasure and understanding that paying close attention to the horse can bestow. The photographs will help you see the horse in a new way so that when you find yourself watching horses in a field, you will be able to read and appreciate the nuances of their behavior. A few of the many breeds found worldwide are featured and I hope that you find your personal favorite among them. Perhaps you will even discover a new favorite, one that you feel especially embodies the spirit of the horse.

Running with the herd

In touch with the wild past

> **In the distance, a rumble. Thunder, maybe. But no—it gets closer, develops a rhythm, remains steady and builds. Then, over the hill, a herd of horses appears, the gold of a low sun behind them. They surge over the green and yellow pasture like a flock of birds through the sky, sharing one instinct but with many hearts pounding as strongly as the hooves. The wind catches their manes and tails, sweat glistens on their burnished coats as they gallop by, swerving around a stand of woodland then sweeping back over the hill and out of sight. But we stand watching for some time, hoping they might come back.**

The power of horses running together stirs a sense of freedom and excitement in us—we find the collective power of animals in a group hugely appealing. The thunder of hooves is an evocative sound, raising adrenalin and inspiring us to scramble for a good view—but from a safe position! No one would risk standing in the way of galloping horses and that collective power sums up much of the strength that the herd offers. A horse alone is vulnerable to predators, but as part of a herd it shares the collective eyes, ears, and instincts of all its companions for protection. The safety of the herd is central to the way horses perceive the world.

When a herd of horses—and to the horse, a herd is any number greater than one—is resting, usually one individual will remain watchful, either standing while others lie down, or lying up on its chest while the others lie out flat. The watch-horse may seem to be dozing too, but it will look up instantly if there is even a slight change in the surroundings. It is a very relaxed group indeed in which one horse does not remain more alert than the others, and this usually only happens when all-round visibility is good. Even domestic horses raised for generations in countries where there are no large predators retain this instinctive sense of watchfulness.

When horses are grazing, if one raises its head or wanders off, the others will soon follow. If they drift apart as they seek the best grass, it is not long before the group re-forms. The sense of unseen communication is strong and the bonds of the group are reinforced by synchronized behavior.

Right: *The playful muzzle-to-muzzle contact shows how at ease these two horses are with one another. The muzzle is one of the most sensitive parts of the horse's body.*

Horses are natural herd animals and need companionship. Everything about them is shaped by their nature and this is one of the reasons why it is not a good idea to keep a horse on its own. A stabled horse may be stressed if kept alone and will be much happier with even a small animal like a cat for company, than if kept in isolation. Out in a field, sheep or cattle as grazing companions are better than life in isolation. But another equine is what is really preferred, and horses can even form strong bonds with a donkey when another horse is not around for companionship.

Mutual grooming, where horses stand head to tail and scratch one another with their teeth, is not only needed for skin care; it is also a significant bonding activity, strengthening the cohesion of the whole herd.

Even though we are used to horses being confined in a field or a stable, or restrained when under saddle or in harness, all their instincts are to avoid restriction for their own safety. More than anything else, horses need to feel safe. They find that sense of security by knowing their place in the herd order. It is easy for us to view this simply as a hierarchy or a pecking order because, as predators ourselves, we understand the instincts of the hunting pack better than we do those of the hunted herd. But herd animals have a different and complex interaction, and the more humans

Opposite: *While this stallion's eye looks relaxed, his posture and the position of his ears show he is calm but alert, as he would be while watching over his mares and foals.*

understand the shifting and changing way in which a herd works, the more able we will be in developing relationships with our own horses and with equines in general.

Safety in numbers

Wild herds are guarded by a stallion who protects his mares and foals, engaging in savage fights with other males who challenge him. But leading the day-to-day life of the herd is the responsibility of experienced mares who have the wisdom to inspire confidence and show leadership. A lead mare makes sure that young horses learn their manners and will drive them away if their behavior threatens the peaceful status quo. Only when they accept their junior position in a respectful way will they be allowed to return. A lead mare will also take the decision to move on in search of new grazing or water.

Within the herd, the order will constantly change depending on the age and character of each individual horse, and this is true of domesticated horses too. Not all horses want to be a leader, but all horses want to be safe and know their own place in the herd structure. Each animal's position in the herd is determined as much by its individual character as its capacity for leadership. So a horse that is not a natural leader may attempt to gain a higher and more secure position in the herd.

For instance, a horse that lacks confidence may be more urgent in its need to move to a secure place, which is usually achieved by asserting itself over weaker or younger horses. But horses do not necessarily fight for their place in the herd. Most of their interaction is based on the confidence to assert themselves within the herd, using nothing more than body language to show their intent. In this way they can avoid confrontation and potential injury.

Horses can behave in a very threatening manner toward one another though serious fights are rare. A warning sign, usually flattened ears, is often enough to prevent confrontation. A horse that is defending itself may turn to kick with the hind legs, whereas one that is asserting itself is likely to lunge forward. This is often alarming to watch, but observing this behavior offers clues as to how we can safely and confidently interact with horses. It is important not to step back if a horse tries to move boldly into your space and push you away—this is not always easy or safe to do, as even a small pony is heavy enough to knock a person over.

When a large, powerful horse moves toward us very quickly, it is instinctive to step back to avoid danger. But this instantly sends out a message that we are not strong enough to hold our position and offer that horse the confident leadership it needs to feel secure. We are signaling

Right: *While some members of the herd relax, others remain on guard. They have chosen an open area in this environment of hills and hollows, where visibility is good all-round.*

that we can be ignored or intimidated, which sets up future problems. Teaching the horse to stand away from us, and being ready to ask it firmly to back up if it gets too close, will restore the balance.

Studies of horses in the wild suggest that domestic herds can often be more tense and aggressive in their interaction. This may be because they are restricted in small paddocks where they cannot move away from one another to avoid confrontation. It may also be because they are kept in gender groups or because the mix of personalities is unbalanced. But when observing horses in any herd over a period of time, it soon becomes clear that the relationships are subtle and complex, revealing instinct, sensitivity, and intelligence. The same horse may not take the lead all the time. The interaction is sometimes hard for us to interpret but, for the horse, it's always about feeling confident and safe in an accepted position within the herd.

It is this need for confident leadership that enables us to form a trusting working relationship with a horse or even a lasting bond. The relationships that horses form with one another and with humans are based entirely on safety and respect. The horses around it will very quickly teach a pushy young horse some manners. This reinforces its place in the herd by reminding it that

Left: *Safety in numbers within the herd structure gives the horse confidence and security. Our aim as handlers and riders is to provide confident leadership so that our horses may willingly accept the partnership we offer.*

as a junior member of the herd it does not inspire other herd members with confidence. A dominant horse may bully its way into a lead position to obtain the best food, for instance, but the herd leader is likely to be a quietly confident individual and, ultimately, that is the horse the others will choose to follow.

So, how can we learn from this when we interact with our horses? If someone is calm, confident, and focused, the horse is more likely to respond willingly because that person is showing leadership. A horse may be bullied into submission and may even choose to cooperate, but that will not build strong foundations for a trusting and lasting partnership. Even a very dominant horse needs to accept a rider's leadership willingly if both parties are to be safe. Forced submission is not the same.

While the idea of wildness may seem exciting and attractive, we would be rightly alarmed if all the latent wildness of our domestic horses was unleashed. So the impression we make on the horse needs to be genuine and lasting to be secure in all situations. If, for instance, the horse becomes afraid, if it lacks genuine trust in its rider to keep it safe, it may rely entirely on its instinct and run away from what it perceives as danger. Therefore, our ability to handle the horse, directing its energy safely and winning its cooperation, is key to our working relationship.

> "The **herd leader** is likely to be a **quietly confident** individual and, **ultimately**, that is the horse the others will **choose to follow**."

Right: *While wild and domestic horses differ in many ways, the instinct of stallions to fight over mares and territory remains the same.*

Wild and domesticated horses differ. Once a wild species becomes domesticated, over the generations it changes; shaped by selective breeding, the regular provision of food, and protection from danger. Some of the wild edges are smoothed over. Male horses are usually castrated at a fairly early age if they are not to be kept for breeding. This makes them more manageable and easier to keep with other horses. Given that the drives of a herd are largely based on the need to breed, we immediately alter the nature of the underlying relationships within the herd.

Yet despite thousands of years of domestication, the basic nature of the horse remains the same. This is why young horses are not born tame or ready to ride, even if they are descended from long lines of domestic stock. We still need to win their confidence, get them used to handling, and train them. Horses learn from other horses, so this process will normally be much easier for a young horse born in a domesticated setting than it is for one captured in the wild with no previous human contact. But it is still essential to train a horse from an early age.

By nature, a horse needs liberty. For survival in the wild a horse relies on its instincts to run away from danger. In a domestic situation this same instinct might drive a frightened horse into a fence or onto a road in panic. Once its attention

is focused on a threat from which it is fleeing, a horse's desire to escape overrides everything else. But, while genuine predators out to kill and eat a domestic horse are rare in most locations, any unfamiliar object or something that moves suddenly, can trigger the flight response. Most horse owners know that a flapping plastic bag can frighten the calmest of horses, especially if it is in a place where there was no plastic bag yesterday or encountered on a ride in an unfamiliar location. All the instincts of the horse warn it to be wary of sudden movements, strange places, unfamiliar shapes or smells that might mean that a predator is lurking. This doesn't mean that the horse is being stupid or difficult—it's reminding us that it feels threatened. Despite centuries of domestication, the horse always remains in touch with the needs and instincts of its wild past.

Left: *The natural instinct of the horse is to run away from danger. Unexpected objects or startling sounds may trigger a flight response if the horse feels threatened.*

Horses are not born tame or **ready to ride**… we still need to **win their confidence**, get them used to **handling**, and **train** them. "

Return to the wild

Today, there is only one truly wild species of horse and that is *Equus ferus przewalskii*, the Asiatic or Mongolian wild horse, also known as Przewalski's horse. Before 1879, this small horse was unknown outside its native territory. Having heard that wild horses still survived on the edge of the Gobi Desert, Russian naturalist and surveyor Colonel Nicolai Przewalski set out to find them. It was thought that they had been hunted to extinction by the nomadic Kirghiz people who wanted them for meat and skins, so the discovery of small herds surviving in isolation caused great excitement.

Sadly, early attempts to save the Przewalski's horse only endangered it further. Many horses were killed during attempts to round them up or died later due to poorly managed captivity. By 1969, there were no Przewalski's horses living wild in Mongolia, and although captive herds were well established in Europe and the United States, they were experiencing problems with inbreeding that put the entire species at risk. Today, however, they are thriving due to carefully managed captive breeding programs. Slowly and carefully, after a long period of acclimatization to independence from humans, they have been returned to their native environment.

In 1998, they were reintroduced to the steppes of Russia and today flourish in the Hustai National Park. While they are protected from human hunters, they must survive natural predators, including wolves, and they depend for survival on all their inherited toughness as the last truly wild horses in the world. The landscape is mountainous, but also has wide open plateaus of rough grassland as well as salt lakes, marshes, and sandy dunes, forests, and glaciers. Extremes of heat and cold, flood and drought in this harsh terrain have shaped these golden horses over thousands of years and will continue to do so now that they have returned home.

Przewalski's horse was initially seen as a direct link between primitive and modern breeds. However, it is now thought to be a distinct species as it has 66 chromosomes, rather than the 64 of the domesticated horse. Like zebras, they are very difficult to tame and can be aggressive, even when bred in captivity. In appearance, they are small, tough horses very similar to the drawings of hunted horses depicted in the earliest cave paintings. Standing 12 to 14 hh (hands high) at maturity, they have long ears, an upright, bristly mane, and a sparse tail. The dorsal stripe, a black line running the length of the spine and extending into the mane and tail, is one of the most noticeable characteristics, along with the sandy gold color of its coat, which varies in shade from season to season.

The physical appearance and complex behavior of the Przewalski's horse (*see* above) is a reminder that the modern horses we know today have been influenced by long years of domestication but still retain a wild heritage and a natural herd instinct.

The wild herds live in groups, known as "harem herds," comprising a lead stallion with his mares and offspring who are not yet ready for breeding. Once the young fillies and colts become sexually mature, they are driven out to fend for themselves. They may join bachelor groups, young horses of both sexes that will eventually separate into new herds, or be allowed to join other "harem herds." In this case, the colts will live on the margins of the herd, keeping a safe distance from the lead

stallion, though in time stronger characters may start to challenge him. These separate herds may all meet at watering places, or as they move from one grazing ground to another, but their interaction is usually peaceful and cautious, unless one stallion should attempt to steal mares from another. Then the stallions will fight fiercely and sometimes even to the death.

When wolves threaten a herd, the mares form a protective circle around the foals and youngsters. The stallion will patrol the perimeter, charging any wolf that gets too close. Mares without foals will not only protect the herd, but also join the stallion in the attack. This is a wonderful example of the strength of the herd, illustrating the capacity of horses to act together for protection.

Legendary horses

Most of the horses considered "wild" today are more accurately described as "feral," as they originally sprang from domestic stock. So, while they have long since shed any domestic influences and are wild in all aspects of their behavior, they do not have the untameable natures of the Przewalski's horse or the zebra. The best-known examples are the American Mustang and the Australian Brumby, though feral horses are found in other parts of the world too.

The Mustang is one of the great symbols of wildness and the frontier spirit of survival. Found across several states of North America, and particularly in Nevada where it was commemorated on the State Quarter coin in 2006, the Mustang roams arid lands composed of highly alkaline soil and scrub grasses that stretch across vast plains rising to rocky peaks. Its history as a horse that has become wild over time adds to its appeal—even its name derives from the Spanish term for "stray," *mesteño.*

It is generally accepted that today's Mustang is descended from escaped or abandoned horses originally brought to the Americas by Spanish explorers in the sixteenth century. The Spanish breeds and types have a long history of resilience and they pass on vital characteristics down the generations. These features have served Mustangs well as they have developed into tough animals, coping with sparse grazing and hard terrain. Averaging around 14 hands in size, they come in many colors—sorrel, or chestnut, bay, and roan are common. The influence of ranch stock and other breeds that were either released or escaped, especially during the nineteenth century, has also shaped them. Famous as cow ponies and the mount of the U.S. Cavalry as well as the Native American tribes, their feisty spirit sums up the grit and endurance that characterizes the North American West.

Legends have grown up around the Mustang and stories of an exceptional white stallion persisted for more than 60 years, long beyond the life expectancy of any single horse. The range over which this horse was said to have roamed also stretched the bounds of credibility as sightings were reported from places as far apart as Texas and Montana. He was reputed to be faster than any other horse, more intelligent in evading capture, and capable of organizing campaigns of military precision to protect his herd against danger. His exploits were even reported in the *New York Times* in 1882. Many Native American tribespeople believed him to be a ghost horse. Substantial prize money was offered to anyone who could capture him alive, but it remained unclaimed. For the sake of both the horse and the legend, this was probably for the best.

"The **Mustang** is one of the great **symbols of wildness** and the frontier **spirit of survival**. "

Right: *White horses are rare and stand out among a herd of mixed colors. This has probably led to the importance of the white horse in legend as a symbol of individuality and independence.*

While this sort of story always owes much to rumor and imagination, tales of the white ghost stallion hint at a core of truth. He was said to have marshaled his mares into a defensive circle against wolves, and the same behavior has been documented by rangers monitoring Przewalski's horses. He was also said to have cooperated with the stallions of other herds, to the extent that he would lead them all in times of danger. This is also behavior documented by naturalists observing wild horse herds.

In the late nineteenth century, when this story captured people's imaginations, the white horse was just one animal among more than a million wild horses roaming the Great Plains. It is likely that several white horses among the roan, gray, and bay horses in the vast herds made a strong impression on travelers. It wouldn't take long for their stories to coalesce into the form of a single animal with mythical qualities, the embodiment of untamed spirit, a wild white ghost stallion.

Yet for all the romance of such legends, the Mustang has long had to endure hardship and persecution. At the turn of the nineteenth century, it was estimated that there were up to two million wild horses in the United States, but by the middle of the twentieth century, there were fewer than 20,000 left. While they have always been hunted for meat or captured to add to domesticated herds,

Opposite: *Mustangs are known as horses of dry terrain, desert, and scrubland, traveling long distances to find food in their sparse environment.*

their speed and agility, as well as knowledge of the native terrain, ensured that enough horses remained free for their numbers to thrive. But once helicopters and motor vehicles were used to round them up, it became harder for them to escape. Soon, greater numbers were culled or slaughtered for meat to protect cattle grazing. Protests against this action and the harsh methods used eventually led to legal protection being granted between the late 1950s and the 1970s. But loopholes in the laws meant that the wild horses continued to be at risk and this danger persists today.

They are seen by some as an indigenous part of the landscape and a key element in the heritage of the American West. Others, however, argue that they are an introduced species, competing for the available food with commercially tended livestock and genuinely wild species. Supporters of the Mustang counter that most of the wild horse herds favor remote, arid areas away from humans. These are less useful for cattle, which need pasture-land and ready access to the water that horses will travel much farther to find. The arguments continue to rage back and forth, and sadly they are often more focused on the commercial issues than the heritage and welfare of the horses.

Today, schemes have been established that encourage the adoption of Mustangs, either to protect them in their native environment or to train them as riding horses. They are readily trainable and excel as working, leisure, and competition horses. But they are at their best when seen galloping in a wild herd, raising clouds of sandy dust, their coats echoing the reds and browns of the desert landscape.

Wild heritage

Like the Mustang, the Australian Brumby is descended from escaped or abandoned imported stock, although it does not have such a long history. The first horses to arrive in Australia were English and Spanish types in the late eighteenth century, followed later by Arabians. The Brumby has also become a symbol of the tough nature and resilience of the pioneer spirit but, in a more poignant parallel, it has also been persecuted and branded a pest.

Opinions differ regarding the origin of the name "Brumby." Some sources believe that it refers to the surname of a man who deliberately released horses into the wild. Others think it comes from an Aboriginal word meaning "wild." These differences of opinion reflect the blurred history of these horses—most of what is known about their past is largely based on hearsay, rather than hard fact. It is certain, however, that for the early pioneers in Australia it was essential to have a horse that could cope with severe climate and poor grazing, while working hard and traveling long distances.

Brumbies come in a **great range** of sizes and colors. They may be **small ponies** or impressively **large horses**.

Any animal that survived to pass on its genes was sure to be of the toughest stock, and those that ended up running wild would be the toughest of all. New blood was introduced when horses intended as cavalry mounts were bred in large numbers in the great open spaces of Australia. Inevitably, many escaped or interbred with existing wild herds.

Later still, horses were released into the wild as they were supplanted by machines for farming and transport purposes. Today, herds of Brumbies, known locally as "mobs" or "bands," live in a remote and challenging environment across wide areas of Australia. Estimates of numbers rarely correlate, but they are found from the deserts of the Northern Territory to the National Parks of central Queensland and New South Wales. In each region, the horses display distinctive physical features depending on the influence of different stock over time.

However, the success of the Brumby has resulted in its persecution. As it is not a native of Australia, it may legally be controlled if it causes a threat to indigenous plants. Regular round-ups for culling have been common for a long time. However, like the Mustang, the Brumby has many supporters and the quick wits and agility of these horses mean they adapt well to being domesticated. They have good temperaments and a reputation for versatility as work or leisure horses. Due to the wide range of breeds that influenced their development, Brumbies come in a great range of sizes and colors. They may be small ponies or impressively large horses. Palominos show up alongside the occasional spotted horse and the more usual chestnut and bay. They all share the capacity to learn and form very strong bonds with their trainers, though they are also known for strength of character and independence of mind, developed as a result of living the rough life of a wild horse.

Water horses

The Mustang and the Brumby are both found in largely arid environments, but there are feral and semiferal horses in wetlands too, including populations in the Danube Delta and the Rhône Delta of southern France, home of the famous Camargue horse.

The Danube Delta in Romania is one of the largest wetland areas in Europe and has UNESCO status as both a Biosphere Reserve and a World Heritage Site. Horses have lived in the delta wetlands for around 350 years and, like many wild herds today, they are thought to have descended from domestic horses that escaped or were released. The delta is an unusual environment containing Europe's largest unbroken expanse of reeds, as well as two unique ancient forests of oak and lianas. It is home to waterbirds, such as cormorants, pelicans, spoonbills, and red-breasted geese, medicinal plants, and fish including the endangered sturgeon. The populations of small stocky horses are usually brown or black; sturdy working types of between 14 and 15 hands. Their breeding success meant that they became a threat to the delicate ecosystem of the delta, where in areas such as the Letea Forest rare plants are carefully protected. As with many wild herds, the harsh methods used to control them meant that they eventually became threatened themselves, until moves were made to protect them.

Today, a restricted breeding program controls numbers, while feed is provided in harsh weather and veterinary care helps to keep the horses strong and healthy. With careful management, the forest and the horses can both thrive as horses contribute to the biodiversity of the woodland.

The Camargue is also a river delta, where the Rhône meets the Mediterranean Sea. It is an area of flat marshes and beaches of fine sand, with sea lavender and tamarisk scenting the salty air and a few lonely trees standing like sentinels watching the sea. Honed by the fierce winds of the mistral, it is hot in summer but very cold in winter; a land of sparkling clear air that may suddenly be swathed completely by sea mists. Through the mists and the reeds, herds of white horses roam freely, splashing through the shallows. The horses of the Camargue are unusual in that they are

thought to have been indigenous to the area for thousands of years. The influence of Barb stock in the seventh and eighth centuries shows in their strong, compact bodies and sharp intelligence. Born black or brown but turning to white-gray as they mature, they have broad hooves adapted to the sand and saltwater environment where they browse on samphire and reeds. Traditionally, they are not shod and stand around 14 hands, although they can carry an adult man easily.

While they have always lived in wild herds, these horses are classed as semiferal as they also have a long working history of domestication, primarily as the horses of the *gardians*, who are responsible for the management of the equally famous black bulls which roam the swamplands as well. The Camargue are perhaps fortunate among the "wild" breeds for their long tradition of working with humans, to which they are well adapted. They are also famous enough to be an important tourist attraction in their own right. Prospects for their long-term success look good because of this link to the commercial prosperity of their native environment.

As well as horses that are truly wild or that have become wild, many breeds are traditionally kept in semiwild herds, even though they have human owners. The viability of this way of life is often linked to the availability of common land, as well as long-standing traditions.

Through the **mists** and the **reeds**, herds of white **Camargue horses** roam freely, **splashing** through the **shallows**.

Mountains and moorlands

In Britain, the open moorlands and mountains of Wales, Scotland, and southern England are all associated with native breeds, some of which are still kept in semiwild herds today.

The ponies of Exmoor in southwest England have roamed the moors for hundreds, maybe even thousands, of years and they are often described as Europe's most ancient breed. They are mentioned in the Doomsday Book, but only as recently as 1818 were records established and breeding programs managed. Many of today's herds still belong to the families that first took part in the initiative to maintain and record the breed.

The landscape has much to do with the tradition of what is called "free-living" for the Exmoor pony. Moorland is windswept, open country with swathes of heather that bears striking purple flowers in late summer. The peaty soil is criss-crossed by shifting paths created by the impact of the rain and high winds. Animals living on moorland need to be able to range widely to live off the nutritionally poor grazing and to find shelter in bad weather. The Exmoor pony lives alongside red deer, as well as rare butterflies, moths, and birds such as the Dartford warbler and the red grouse. The ponies echo the colors of a winter moorland—they are classed as bay, but they range from reddish-brown to dark brown through to lighter dun, always with a distinctive mealy color on their muzzles, around their hooded eyes, and on their bellies. They have thick black manes and tails that help to protect them from the wild moorland weather as do their two-layered winter coats.

The Exmoor is a small and sturdy animal, only reaching around 12 hands but with an elegant head and neat, strong limbs. One of the most unusual features of the breed is that it has developed naturally, shaped by its environment. Because it lives in isolation, it has not been greatly influenced by outside stock, unlike breeds which have been very carefully developed through breeding programs. The shape of its jaw is unusual, with traces of a seventh molar not found in any other modern breed.

The herds run wild on the moor for most of the year but owners round up their ponies in the fall for medical checks, branding, and microchipping. Any that are to be weaned, sold, or selected for training are kept back, while the others are released again. The moor has shaped the characteristics of these ponies, but the ponies have also helped to shape the moor as their grazing keeps down scrub, allowing more delicate plants and flowers to thrive. They are part of Exmoor's essential character and the semiwild foundation stock is vital to maintain the breed, which is classed as endangered by the Rare Breeds Survival Trust.

Exmoors make excellent children's ponies, having native intelligence, sure feet, and wits honed by their hard environment, so there is demand for them in the working world of the domestic horse. But to maintain that spirit, the foundation stock must always be maintained and cherished, so that they continue to move easily among the gorse bushes; shadowy shapes with manes like tussocks of grass, drifting among the mists and shifting paths of the open moor.

Not far away, the ponies of Dartmoor share many of the characteristics of moorland breeds, being small, hardy, and sure-footed. But they do not boast such a long history and, up until the nineteenth century, the genetic line was regularly influenced by outside blood. The Dartmoor pony is slightly taller than the Exmoor and does not share its mealy coloring. Black, brown, or bay are the usual colors. These ponies have well-shaped heads and limbs, with a refinement that makes them popular show ponies for children.

Out on the moor, they grow strong and fit all summer before they are gathered in during the fall round-ups, known as "drifts." All the ponies are sorted into holding pens by their respective owners and identified by a brand or particular cut of the tail, in preparation for sale at auction.

These ponies have suffered from changes over time and are also considered vulnerable as a rare breed. Conservation grazing is one of the innovations set up by The Dartmoor Pony Heritage Trust to help them survive. This promotes the ponies as ecologically useful in land management, as they are selective grazers and help to maintain biodiversity. Their grazing habits help to preserve the open vegetation, which is essential to the survival of many rare species of moorland plants. They also restrict the spread of bracken by trampling down young fronds in spring and the dead plants in winter, which allows more delicate plants to grow through and thrive. These grazing habits can be beneficial in other landscapes too, so the Dartmoor pony may be useful away from its native habitat, a characteristic that should help to consolidate the breed's future.

The New Forest, Hampshire, in the far south of England, is one of the few places in the United Kingdom where it is possible to observe free-roaming horses at fairly close hand. The ponies that live there all belong to New Forest Commoners, local residents who have grazing rights in the forest and surrounding open land. To be registered as Forest Bred, the ponies have to be born in the forest. They are found in a range of solid colors, especially bay and other brown shades. They are small and tough, and, like the Exmoor pony that lives not far away, have a history older than any written records can reveal.

In the New Forest you may see ponies of all ages interacting in a relaxed way. While they are not exactly wild, neither are they constrained in fields and subject to daily handling as most domestic horses are. Newborn foals and youngsters can be seen living in a herd environment, until such time as the colts are taken away to prevent them breeding. Unusually though, while they are free-living like the Exmoor and Dartmoor ponies, New Forest ponies are known for their relaxed attitude around people. They are often seen wandering around villages in the forest or begging from picnicking tourists. Even when they are overly familiar, they should be treated with caution and never offered food. But their relative confidence with humans makes them interesting to observe from a safe distance.

The idea of horses running wild may delight the horse lover, conjuring up a link to a romantic past and the spirit of freedom. However, it is a complicated issue. Horses that are classified as "wild" today, those that do not have legal owners, often find themselves threatened or considered as a nuisance. Horses—even relatively small ponies—are large animals, and wildness is a hard condition to manage. Many wild or semiwild breeds are at risk either from loss of habitat, because they are seen as a pest, or because they have no commercial value.

But horses that live in large herds, surviving the changing seasons, develop strength and resilience. All the breeds described in this chapter live in difficult environments, whether hot or cold, wet or dry. They are all physically tough and feisty. They live on sparse grazing and struggle

through difficult winters. This challenging life hones some of the instinctive skills that can be dulled when horses are kept in isolation or with limited access to grazing. Wild horses understand the ways of the herd and instinctively trust confident leadership, are alert to danger, and naturally conserve their energy. This makes them very attractive as working horses, prized for their sure-footededness and intelligence.

Most of the wild or feral horses around the world survive partly because they live in isolated locations (*see* above), whether they are on the Great Plains of North America, the remote steppes of Mongolia, or the boggy moorlands of Britain. Contact with humans can potentially create serious problems for them, but humans usually offer a lifeline too. Many people are dedicated to ensuring

that wild horses continue to enjoy the life of a free-running herd. Once numerous, today wild horses are much harder to see, but it is important to us to know that they are still there, their steps echoing the hoof beats of their ancestors in a modern world where true wildness is constantly being eroded.

As for domestic horses, their wild ancestry means that the herd is the place in which they are happiest. So when we see horses grazing in a field, usually covered in mud and looking relaxed, we can be sure that this is as close to their natural environment as they can be. When we interact with them, we should draw on our understanding of the herd and the sense of security that calm, confident leadership bestows, to make training and riding more enjoyable for both horse and rider alike.

The spiritual horse

Folklore, myths, and legends

> **❝** Again we hear the thunder of hooves, but these horses are not just running for fun. Something has caught their attention and their heads are up, nostrils flaring, sensing something we cannot see. They charge up a small hill and whirl round to stand poised, some snorting, ears pricked, all focused on the middle distance. Then it's over. The lead horse shakes her head and buckles at the knees to roll, others roll too, then they all stand and start to graze, the excitement of the moment now forgotten. A youngster, not so ready to relax, prances and high-steps around its mother, tail held like a plume, before tucking in behind her flank. **❞**

The spirit of the horse, its essential nature, has the power to move us, even if we do not fully understand why. There is something in a horse's eye, the set of its head, its alertness or even its relaxed demeanor that catches the attention. Horses can move faster than we can ever hope to, the wind in their manes, the open landscape unfolding under their hooves. They conjure up dreams of wildness and freedom, the romance of riding into the sunset, the thrill of the pioneer trail, the excitement of the daring leap, the risk of the wide river crossing. We don't need to know much about horses to appreciate that they have power and strength to which we can never aspire, and which we find inspirational.

On horseback, humans have undertaken seemingly impossible journeys and while that says a lot about the human spirit, the significance of the equine spirit must not be underestimated either. But what do we really mean by spirit? It is not just the combined physical abilities of the horse, or even the individual character that every horse undoubtedly possesses. That indefinable quality that makes a horse different from any other animal has inspired writers, artists, and storytellers since time immemorial.

Much of what we define as "spirit" in the horse relates to its sensitivity. It has subtle and acute senses that, as a prey animal, it relies on for survival. Horses have a group identity and, in some respects, a group consciousness that makes them alert and sensitive to the moods of their companions or their human handler. A horse is able to sense if a rider is confident or apprehensive,

truly relaxed or only pretending to be so. A horse that knows someone well can also tell if they are upset, grieving, or emotionally agitated and all of these moods influence the safety of the human/horse partnership.

A bold horse may be willing to take charge and set out confidently, but a nervous one will become more shy, more nervous, needing the rider to take the reins, both literally and figuratively. This sort of subtlety is what makes the spirit of the horse so deeply engaging—the horse reflects its handler and we recognize our strengths and weaknesses by the way in which our horse responds to us.

Horses love to run (*see* above). Their pleasure in the capacity for speed is evident when they are at liberty with their companions, all tearing around a field together for no apparent reason. They reveal high spirits when leaping and playing, chasing one another and playfighting. In the same way, when they are afraid or rebellious, they express

themselves through movement and energy. It is exciting to revel in the power and speed of horses and the thrill of riding a fast horse is perhaps the closest we can get to the sensation of flying. But it can be frightening too and the risk involved in trusting a large, fast-moving animal is part of the overall elation that we feel.

Once we connect with the spirit of the horse to create a partnership, this experience is heightened further. It is small wonder that riders across the world have always aspired to a sense of oneness with the horse. The capacity for athletic movement and speed is channeled by humans into racing, showjumping, and endurance riding, as well as riding simply for the joy of it. A horse that is fully engaged with the partnership too will give of its best and willingly run faster, leap higher, and keep going for longer. These are the unique relationships that go far beyond training or technique and become inspirational.

Opposite: *The energy in this horse leaping with all four hooves off the ground is refined and channeled in the highly controlled movements of classical dressage.*

However, if a horse is said to be "spirited," this has quite a different meaning and it is not always a positive description. Anyone looking to buy a horse knows that an advertisement for a "spirited" horse often means one that's a challenge! The term "spirited" usually implies that a horse has a strong will, and so is unlikely to be suitable for a novice or a rider lacking confidence. In the past, when controlling a horse was seen as a metaphor for self-discipline, the ability to master a spirited horse was a kind of test—the more difficult the horse was, the bigger and better the challenge. But this attitude is linked to notions of dominance and mastery that are much less attractive to the modern rider. Today, there is more focus on building a cooperative relationship with the horse, of being a confident, but not dominating, leader with a relaxed and considerate approach. The image of a horse with rolling eyes, fighting a fierce bit, resisting the rider and eventually submitting to a more powerful human will is part of a much older tradition.

Instead of viewing a spirited horse as an animal to overcome, an accomplished rider today is more likely to see this characteristic as potential that may be channeled into performance. The spirited horse is the choice for those who want to go far, to move boldly, forming a partnership with a worthy companion that will both lead and follow when required. When riding a spirited horse, for example, the rider can confidently hand over the responsibility for traversing dangerous ground, safe in the knowledge that the horse has enough common sense and intelligence to find a safe route. On this sort of horse, the rider can ask for more effort when faced with an emergency or against the clock in a competitive situation and be certain that the horse will respond accordingly.

This does not mean that quiet or gentle horses lack spirit, rather it implies that they have a softer quality. These are the companions we trust with our children, or that give confidence to novice riders; the ones we choose for a relaxed ride around country tracks, reliable enough to provide therapy through riding for disabled people or to take part in personal development programs for young people. They are often gentle cobs with soft eyes and patient natures, hairy fetlocks, and full manes, or older experienced horses that have seen and done it all. They can usually rise to the occasion for a good gallop but will settle down again quickly.

One of the most wonderful aspects of the horse is its capacity to understand and protect people. Even a horse with the fieriest spirit can show gentleness toward a child, and there are many reports of horses defending their human companion, going for help in an emergency, or alerting people to a fire or a coming storm.

positive energies, good fortune, and the journey to enlightenment. At a deeper level, it is linked to the element of space and is the pivotal figure through which the other elements of wind, earth, fire, and water, all represented by animals, interact. At the deepest level, it represents the subtle energy or life force of the body on which the mind rides, guiding and controlling the thoughts. Tibetan prayer flags, also known as "windhorses," often carry images of five animals: the tiger, the snow lion, the birdlike *garuda,* and the dragon in the four corners, with stories and folklore too.

In classical Greek mythology, the sea-god Poseidon was challenged by the goddess Demeter to create the most beautiful creature ever seen. He created the horse, forming it from breaking waves. Like other gods, Poseidon often assumed the form of a horse himself. It was an appropriate disguise, as to the Ancient Greeks the horse symbolized potency, majesty, loyalty, and wisdom. Immortal horses feature prominently in Greek myth as gifts, creations, and offspring of the gods.

Left: *The link between horses and the elements is enhanced by their speed and sense of wild potential. Like the wind and rain, they are never wholly predictable, even when we think we understand them.*

Athena, goddess of wisdom, is credited with inventing the bit, symbolizing the need for control in her role as guardian of the civilized world.

Teams of horses thunder across the heavens, pulling the chariots of the sun and moon, dawn and night in Greek, Roman, Norse, Iranian, and Hindu mythologies. They are famed for their shining coats, the sound of their hooves and their impressive speed in managing the safe passage from day to night. The sweat dripping from the mane or the bridle of the horse pulling the chariot of night in Scandinavian mythology creates the morning dew. In the Indian Vedic tradition, the sun-god's bride travels in a bridal carriage representing her spirit, covered in a canopy representing heaven, and pulled steadily by two horses to meet her husband.

In old German and Norse tradition, it is the sun-goddess who travels in her chariot, the sun itself, across the heavens, drawn by two horses, with bellows at their shoulders to help cool them in their work.

The speed of the horse has often given rise to creation stories that link it to the elements. In one Islamic tradition, Allah created the horse by commanding the south wind to condense; in some versions he cupped the resultant mist in his hand to breathe life into the creature.

> **"** Teams of **horses thunder** across the **heavens**, pulling the **chariots** of the sun and moon, dawn and night. **"**

Right: *Legend has it that the beautiful Arabian horse was created by the breath of Allah on the condensed essence of the south wind and that it was blessed with the ability to fly without wings.*

Allah placed a star in the center of its forehead to bless the horse with power, good fortune, fertility, and the ability to fly without wings.

In a similar story, the angel Jibril or Gabriel created the horse from a thundercloud, while there are versions that link the two with the angel bringing a handful of the condensed wind to Allah to fashion into a horse.

Arabian spirit

The Arabian horse is particularly associated with myths, legends, and the idea of spirit. The Prophet Muhammad was said to have chosen the mares to become the foundation of his herd by testing their loyalty. After a long journey through the desert, his horses were tired and thirsty and headed gladly toward an oasis where water glimmered. As they gathered speed in relief at the opportunity to drink, the Prophet called them back to him. Five ignored their thirst to return to him and these were the chosen ones. He marked them by pressing his thumb into their necks, leaving a whorl of hair as a mark of their loyalty.

Left: *The distinctive characteristics of an Arabian horse—the dished face, finely shaped ears, sculpted muzzle, and expressive eyes—beautifully complement the wild romance of its carriage and beauty.*

The character of the Arabian horse has a particularly spiritual quality. It is the breed that seems to epitomize the glamor of the horse in an exceptionally beautiful and refined way. Known for delicate features but also great strength and powers of endurance, the distinctive, dished face of Arabian horses makes them easy to recognize.

They have a history that stretches back at least 2,000 years and horses of an Arabian type can be identified in images from even earlier times. The great love that the Bedouin people felt for their horses led to the Arabian being treated as a member of the family, allowed to shelter from desert storms in the tents alongside the children. This care engendered a gentle nature in the breed, allied with great intelligence and an affinity with humans. As it was believed that Allah created and blessed the first horse, treating them with particular care was seen as vital. The bulge of the forehead, the "jibbah" was said to hold the blessing of Allah. The arched and crested neck—the "mitbah"—showed courage, while the high tail carriage was expressive of pride. Mares were especially prized—they were ridden into war, as they were less likely than stallions to be distracted or to call out to the enemy's horses, while still being endowed with impressive courage and spirit.

> The **Arabian horse** has a particularly **spiritual quality**. It epitomizes the **glamor** of the horse in an exceptionally **beautiful** and **refined** way.

Right: *The Arabian horse's fiery spirit, sensitivity, and reactive nature are tempered by its equally famous gentleness and intelligence.*

Five pureblooded lines, known as the *Asil*, were established by selective breeding. Each was different. The *Kehilan* strain was tall, around 15 hh with impressive depth of chest and power, while the *Seglawi* was smaller and especially graceful. The *Hadban* was small too, but strong-boned and very gentle. The *Hamdani* was the tallest, being up to 15.2 hh, with a straighter profile, and the *Abeyan* had longer backs and a higher proportion of gray horses. These five bloodlines were said to be traceable back to the five loyal mares marked by the Prophet. Among the nomadic desert people, breeding records were kept as part of an oral tradition for many hundreds of years, with the pedigrees being traced through the female line.

The Arabian horse is famous because of its ancient lines, its link to the culture of its native people, and its natural characteristics, which include a fine and sensitive spirit. Today, it is well established in many riding disciplines and is the most popular breed for competitive Endurance Riding. Its development in the hard desert terrain, its keen intelligence, and its willing partnership with humans makes it perfectly suited for long, challenging rides.

Opposite: *In legends, the ghost stallion is the symbol of wisdom and resilience, as well as a teacher of hard lessons to humans who lack kindness or generosity.*

White stallions

While Arabian horses come in many colors, the gray has a particularly otherworldly quality and gray or white horses often appear in legend, perhaps for this reason. White horses have long assumed a symbolic importance in myth, religion, and even popular culture around the world.

They are often linked with purity or innocence, carrying heroes in their fight against evil deeds or representing inspiration and creativity. White horses were sacred in many cultures, being worshiped and sometimes even sacrificed. In Native American Blackfoot mythology, the snow-deity rides a white horse, and one of the horses of the Navajo sun-god is made of white shell, and scatters particles of glittering sand and sacred pollen that he offers to the god when he gallops or rolls and shakes himself.

In the stories of the Yinnuwok people of the far north of Canada, an old white horse was the means by which a greedy and cruel man was taught a salutary lesson. This man was jealously devoted to his herd of horses, but only while they were young and strong. When they grew old or fell ill, he treated them cruelly. One day, a strange horse, a broken-down old white stallion, joined his herd. Furious because it was thin and ugly, he beat it savagely and left it to die. He returned hours later, planning to skin the horse for its hide. To his surprise, it had gone.

But that night he saw the old horse in a dream. Little by little, its ancient body grew strong and it was transformed into the most beautiful horse ever, a Ghost Stallion with a shining mane, snow-white coat, and flowing tail. "If you had treated me kindly," the horse told the man, "I would have brought you many horses. Now, because you were cruel, I shall take away all your horses."

When the man awoke, his horses were gone, and though he searched high and low, he could find no sign of them. As he slept, exhausted, the Ghost Stallion appeared to him again and said, "If you wish to find your horses, you must walk for two more days and sleep for two more nights. They are in the hills to the east." The man walked on, but could never catch up with them. Each night the Ghost Stallion encouraged him, telling him that his horses were nearby, but the following day he searched in vain.

He never found them, wandering for his whole lifetime, too greedy to let them go, too proud to admit he'd been wrong. It is said that on a still night, if you hear the drumming of hooves and the shuffling of weary feet, then you know they have passed close by but you mustn't look, because to catch sight of that futile pursuit will bring bad luck.

Dark storms

In many cultures black horses are represented as the mounts of Death. They are also often linked with villainy or evil deeds. However, black horses can also represent achievement, courage, and wisdom.

In a legend of the Yaqui people, Native Americans from Arizona, the great leap of a black horse enabled his rider to pierce a cloud with a spear. The downpour that followed not only quenched their terrible thirst but also guaranteed a supply of water to the area for all time. The Navajo sun-god has horses of turquoise, shell and pearl but he chooses his horse of coal when the sky is dark and stormy.

The association between the color black and storms is well established in many cultures—this additional association with the power of a horse is perfectly understandable. Black horses play an important role in the legend of the Wild Hunt, a tale of ghosts, heroes and fiery steeds that is thought to have Norse roots. There are many variations on the story but in each version a ghostly leader, followed by a chaotic band of hounds and riders, hurtles through the night, creating a tumult of thunder, howling, and raging winds.

The black horses of the Wild Hunt are alarmingly supernatural. They have eyes like red-hot coals and churn up the land with the pounding of their flaming hooves. They leave devastation in their wake and cause storms in the sky. The horses may also lack limbs or heads, and bear wounds or the effects of age and ill-use. In a traditional mummer's play from Yorkshire, the Huntsman's horse sings a song of willing sacrifice, offering to be ridden to death so that he can join the Wild Hunt.

The links already seen between darkness, black horses, and death are strong as the Wild Hunt presages war, destruction, or pestilence.

The Norse god Odin's horse, Sleipnir, has eight legs; these are thought to represent the legs of four men carrying a bier to a funeral. In this guise, Odin and Sleipner are gatherers of the dead. In other versions of the story, historical or semi-historical figures, such as the Emperor Charlemagne and King Arthur, are the leaders of the hunt.

The horses of the Wild Hunt gallop on nights associated with festivals of the dead or changing seasons, such as Yuletide and New Year. In Norway, it was customary to leave out a sheaf of corn or a measure of grain for the Huntsman's horse, to ensure plenty in the time to come. Young men would often dress up and re-enact the hunt, being given similar gifts of feed for their horses to ensure prosperity. This legend bears an added menace, as anyone who did not observe it would be punished for ignoring the tradition and thereby risked incurring bad luck for the whole community.

Right: *The Spanish horse shaped Renaissance culture when the noble qualities of the rider were tested in his ability to ride a spirited horse in a way that displayed its natural grace.*

Iberian beauty

The horses of Spain are the archetypes of the majestic horse. With rippling manes and compact, rounded bodies, they carry themselves as though aware of their own beauty. Their presence and fiery spirit have made them the choice of kings throughout Europe since the early Renaissance. To own one was a measure of status for any nobleman, as they were costly and difficult to obtain outside their native lands, partly because their breeders were loath to part with them. A high price ensured that only wealthy people might own one. In the seventeenth century, an English lord would need a team of around half a dozen men, including grooms, farriers, and guards to protect against theft, in order to collect a single horse from Spain.

A nobleman was not only expected to display his spirit and gracious bearing on the battlefield, but also in the socially competitive world of the court. Riding as an art allowed a man to show leadership and physical skill, and the Spanish horse—compact, elegant, and full of character— was the ideal choice. When the foundations of dressage were being laid down in riding houses— elegant buildings designed solely for the pursuit of the art of horsemanship—these were the horses that excelled. They were intelligent, highly trainable, and elegant in their movements.

Their physical features include natural collection, due to the level of flexion possible in the hind legs, which provides the necessary athleticism to perform the "high airs," great leaps where all four hooves leave the ground.

One of the great horsemen of the time was William Cavendish, 1st Duke of Newcastle, who lived from 1593 to 1676. A passionate rider from boyhood to old age, he was devoted to the Spanish horse for its beauty, spirit, and intelligence. Among his many stories of fine horses, he recalled that during one display his horse leapt so high and whirled so fast that he felt dizzy. His horses were so responsive that he rode one with only a scarf around its neck and at the end of the performance some noble Spanish visitors to his riding house cried out that to see him ride was miraculous.

The Duke valued Spanish horses as the noblest of their kind and observed that the only problem with them was that they were so intelligent that they could out-think their rider. When a nobleman sent a servant to buy one of Newcastle's horses, he was dismissed without the horse but with the message that the price offered was only half what the great stallion was worth. Newcastle also added that, by the following day, the price would have doubled and by the next, it would have tripled. In short, his horse was not for sale.

Spanish "leaping horses," as they were known then, were costly and required great skill and commitment to train. But according to the Duke of Newcastle, once trained they could be ridden for pleasure, on journeys, or to war with equal confidence. Indeed, he proudly related that a visitor to his riding house told him that his horses lacked nothing but the power of speech to make them as "reasonable" as a human. At a time when animals were thought to lack the power of reason entirely, this was high praise. Newcastle was among the first writers on horses to argue that horses had memory, a great capacity for learning, and well-developed powers of reasoning. He believed that horses should be trained like children, quietly, with regular short lessons, and with a firm, but not violent, hand.

Opposite: *Like many desert horses, the spirit and presence of the Spanish horse seem to reflect the dazzling sun and fierce heat of its native country.*

"With **rippling manes** and compact, rounded bodies, **Spanish horses** carry themselves as though **aware** of their own **beauty**."

Right: *The desert breeds also consistently show the gentle nature expressed by the composed posture of this Lusitano stallion.*

The Spanish horse has been a consistent performer in the art of classical riding throughout its history. The Spanish Riding School of Vienna is so-named because it was founded on Spanish horses in the late sixteenth century. The famous Lipizzaners ridden there today were developed during the eighteenth century from nine carefully chosen Spanish stallions and 24 mares. The Lusitano of Portugal is another closely related breed, developed to be slightly taller, while the Alter Real, another Portuguese relation, was developed to maintain the baroque type of horse so perfectly suited to classical riding in its most advanced form.

While Andalusia today refers to a province of southern Spain, centuries ago at the time of the Moorish occupation, the name referred to almost the whole Iberian peninsula. So, while the Spanish horse is often called an Andalusian outside its native country, the Spanish Breeder's Association decided in 1912 that *Pura Raza Española* (Pure Spanish Breed), was a more accurate name.

Spirited, spiritual—the spirit of the horse is difficult to define and impossible to pin down. But what is clear is that the importance of horses in legends, myths, and folk tales from around the world is significant. They impact deeply upon humans on many levels. To storytellers, shamans and truth-seekers of all sorts, this essential connection needs exploration. All the ideas, stories, and beliefs that have grown up around this creature reveal one certain thing: at the deepest level of our being, humans need the horse.

Left: *Our inability to put a finger on just what "spirit" really means in connection with horses is part of the reason we are drawn to them.*

The physical horse
The power and the beauty

> **❝** The horses are relaxing under the trees, tails swishing, eyes half-closed, content to let us wander among them. We speak quietly before stroking their rounded quarters and the long line of their necks, sensing the relaxed potential of their muscles. One mare is more alert than the others, keeping a quiet eye on the surroundings. She's aware of us standing to one side of her and turns her head to get a better look as we stroke her foal, charmed by his whiskery chin. But she knows that we pose no threat and so returns to her casual state of watchfulness, the ear tipped slightly toward us—the only sign that she's still on her guard. **❞**

The physical presence of horses is extremely impressive—their muscular strength, flowing manes and tails, and finely shaped bodies cannot fail to make an impact on us. Among the largest of our domesticated animals, the horse uniquely combines power, beauty, and an inherently amiable nature in one animal. These characteristics mean that we build special relationships with horses. Some may simply inspire us while viewed from a distance, while others are close partners fulfilling a vital working role or participating in many of our leisure activities. They frequently become a valued member of the family too. The close relationship that can form between a comparatively fragile human and a large, powerful animal is one of the most intriguing and inspiring aspects of human cultural history. The nature and spirit of the horse form a crucial element in this partnership, but its complex physical attributes are equally important.

The horse is a grazing and browsing animal equipped with teeth that can both crop and grind. Its eyes are set high up in its long skull so that it can watch for danger while grazing, and the ears are positioned on top of the head so it can hear clearly while the head is lowered. A lining of fine fur stops foreign objects from getting inside the ear, and the soft muzzle is covered with fine hairs that help it to nose out the best choice of grazing. Sensitive to smell, a horse can detect the scent of water from many miles away, and will react strongly to unfamiliar smells, especially those that suggest a predator may be nearby. Horses usually escape from danger by running away and the shape

of their hooves allows them to run swiftly over varied terrain. Long legs with a relatively simple bone structure and a single hoof have evolved for speed, while acute senses mean that a horse is highly aware of its surroundings and always poised for rapid movement, powered by large muscles that are concentrated high on its body to provide speed and agility.

As with most social animals, the posture of the horse reflects its state of mind. The slightest movement of an ear is enough to allow another horse to read and understand the signal. The outer ear is made of cartilage and shaped like a funnel to capture sounds over a wide range at both higher and lower frequencies than humans can hear. As the ears can move independently, they can pick up sounds from different directions at the same time. The ears reveal a horse's state of attentiveness and mood in a way that anyone working with horses can come to rely on as an accurate indicator.

It is commonly believed that if the ears are pointing forward it means a horse is in a good mood and if they are pointing back it indicates a bad mood. However, this is not necessarily the case because the situation is a lot more complex than that. A horse with its ears pricked forward is paying attention to what is ahead—but if its head is also high, it may be alarmed or unsure of what it is hearing. The horse's ear can swivel

in all directions to pick up sounds and it's not unusual to see a horse with one ear pointing forward and one back, indicating that its attention is divided. While a horse may lay its ears back to show anger, it also turns them half-back to listen or to demonstrate submission. The ears may also fall back softly or sometimes to the side if the horse is dozing, but this is a relaxed movement, very different from the appearance of a horse with ears flattened in anger or fear.

The tail is also a good indicator of mood—like the ears, the position of the tail alters the overall shape of the horse. Body posture is a useful method of communication that can inform or alert another horse at a distance. A high tail position usually indicates excitement—though this can mean high spirits or alarm, or it may be part of mating behavior in both males and females. It can also indicate that a horse is about to run away, which gave rise to the saying, "to high-tail it out of here." A relaxed tail indicates a relaxed horse, but a tail that is tucked in may be a sign of fear or defensiveness, or may show that a horse is unwell or feels intimidated and might be about to kick. A swishing tail can mean that the horse is simply keeping troublesome flies away, but it can also be a sign of irritation or annoyance, as well as of discomfort. When a horse is ridden, a swishing tail and irritable demeanor may indicate poorly

Right: *These Camargue horses are very relaxed with one another, as well as their surroundings. The way one horse is curved around the other shows respect for its space and the confidence to be very close.*

fitting or uncomfortable tack, or an underlying physical problem that is painful or preventing the horse from relaxing while working. With most of these signals, the degree of tension is the clue as to whether or not they are casual behavior, warning signs, or the expression of physical discomfort.

Body posture influences the outline of the horse and sends a clear visual signal to other horses in the vicinity. Head tossing or head jerking may lead to rearing which reveals frustration and fear, while neck wringing is an unhappy, irritated movement, usually seen when a horse is not bold enough to vent real anger. When both the head and tail are raised, it results in a curved body shape and high-stepping movement which indicate excitement, whereas low, moderate movements reflect calmness and relaxation—signals to which both horses and humans will react instinctively.

A relaxed horse stands with eyes half-closed, head almost level with or slightly below the withers (the point of the shoulder) and a soft outline, often resting on one hip with the opposite toe on the ground. Once the relaxation turns into dozing, the stifle joint (which is the equivalent of the human knee joint) in the supporting leg will lock so the horse doesn't fall over. This locking is maintained by the action of ligaments in the stifle joint that the horse can activate by rotating its patella (or kneecap).

Body posture influences the outline of the horse and sends a **clear visual signal** to **other horses** in the vicinity.

Natural agility

The movements of classical dressage, especially the airs-above-the-ground, are based on the actions and posturing of stallions, either displaying to mares or showing off to impress a rival. The muscles swell and the neck arches, while the hooves are lifted high. The stallion appears to float over the ground as he prances to show off his mettle and presence. While this male posturing is part of specific stallion behavior, mares and geldings can behave like this too when excited, for example, by the sound of other horses galloping or calling.

Turning to kick is a defensive movement and can involve both hind legs, something often seen in domestic groups where space is limited. A horse that is not strong enough to stand up to a casual bully, but that has enough confidence to protest at being pushed around, will often kick up both back legs. You may see this when horses are larking around, which they often do as youngsters. However, a serious double-barrelled hind-leg kick is something to be reckoned with. It is clear that horses moderate their responses to match the overall mood of the confrontation.

When getting to know one another, or if reunited with an old friend, horses will usually roll, gallop around together, prance and playfight, often to the accompaniment of a lot of noisy squealing as they touch nose-to-nose and breathe on each other. Sniffing with first one nostril, then the other, indicates that they are deciphering the smell in different parts of their brain. They may do this to select foodstuff, locate danger, when bonding, or in mating behavior. If a scent confuses them or arouses especial interest, they may curl the upper lip back, while stretching out the head and neck. It is believed that this action, known as *flehmen*, allows them to get a better understanding of the smell and any associated pheromones. They do this by breathing deeper into the olfactory organ that is located above the roof of the mouth via a duct just behind the front teeth.

Opposite: *This is the sort of buck that would send most riders flying! Yet the potential for the impressive leaps of classical dressage is evident here too.*

We can ride horses comfortably and without causing them injury because of their skeletal and muscular structure. A rider sits on a complex raft of long, powerful muscles and ligaments that protect the horse's spine. But these evolved for running, not for bearing weight, so it is vital to the horse's health to distribute our weight evenly with a well-fitting saddle, a balanced riding position, and correct training.

The horse's back is like a bridge between the front and hindquarters, made up of the spinal vertebrae, additional small joints, ligaments and powerful abdominal muscles. This configuration gives the back stability, but not a lot of flexibility. By contrast, the cervical vertebrae, suspended deep below the topline of the neck, are very flexible, having evolved to allow the horse to stretch its head up into trees, graze low on the ground, and undertake self-grooming.

As a horse is trained, the long muscles of its neck help to counterbalance the additional weight of the rider, but the horse also needs to be actively working its back and hindquarters. Then the neck will lower and round naturally as the horse strides forward, lifting its back muscles and so better supporting the weight of the rider. A horse cannot be forced into balance by the reins, so a horse which is overbent by a strong hand will never move as efficiently or as beautifully as it might.

It may also be at risk of developing an injury because of uneven muscle development, and seem uncomfortable and restless.

When a horse is moving in a relaxed way, carrying its own weight evenly, it will be naturally balanced (*see* above). We attempt to recreate this condition when the additional weight of a rider is added. A horse does not toss its head up and down or champ its teeth together unless it is unhappy—and the same applies when it is being ridden.

When a horse is pulling a heavy cart or a plow, it moves in a different way. It needs to throw its weight forward into the harness and bring the hind legs well under its body, as it would when moving uphill. By looking at the way the horse moves when unencumbered, we can start to determine the best way to help it pull a carriage or carry a load safely.

The size of a horse's chest, body, and legs enable it to carry or pull with speed and stamina. But those features also evolved for survival.

Long legs enable the horse to instinctively run from danger or wander through tall grasslands without its vision being impeded. A deep chest accommodates the large heart and lungs needed to cope with the demands of sudden speed, while the size of its abdomen means it can graze on plants that require a lot of digesting. Ruminants, like cows or sheep, have several compartments in their stomachs. This enables plant food to be partly digested before the cud is regurgitated for further chewing to break it down into digestible matter. Horses, however, only have one stomach and need to trickle-feed, continually taking in small amounts of food, with only a few short rest periods when they are not eating. For this reason, three feeds a day and long periods of gut inactivity while standing in a stable is a bad regime for a domesticated horse. It can result in a painful gastrointestinal condition called "colic," which may be fatal, or complex metabolic disorders.

Most modern pasture was created for grazing cattle or sheep and it is usually too rich for horses. Horses evolved naturally on fairly sparse pastures and so sudden exposure to plentiful lush grass can cause digestive overload, leading to problems including colic and laminitis (inflammation in the hoof). Therefore, even when they can graze freely all day, they can still develop health problems.

The ideal environment for horses is one in which they can browse on a wide range of shrubs, herbs, and trees, as well as grasses, allowing them to forage widely to achieve a balanced diet. The most useful terrain for them will include hard, soft, and stony ground to condition hooves. Free-running water should be available as well as shelter from inclement weather. Providing this combination of features can prove a tall order for many owners, but an awareness of the ideal set-up does help us to make the most of what we do have so that we can keep our horses in good health.

Right: *This lovely Arabian seems to enjoy life in an environment that is close to ideal—rough grass that is plentiful but not lush, with shrubs to browse on and trees for shelter.*

Left: *All breeds develop a thicker coat during the winter, but those from cold climates are especially well provided for. Not only their coats, but their manes, tails, and hair around their legs will protect them from the cold.*

All seasons

A gleaming summer coat is one of a horse's most attractive features, indicating good condition and well-being. But horses change their coat over the seasons, and that shining summer vision may well turn into a shaggy mud-covered mess in the winter. This is exactly the way it should be—the horse is adaptable and indeed this is one of the reasons that it is so successful. Breeds from hot or dry climates have finer hair; they will still develop a winter coat, but its depth and thickness will be significantly less than in breeds from harsher climates that need protection from rain, snow, and cold.

It is quite common for horses to have a long and shaggy winter coat, and while many owners choose to rug horses, their natural protection against the weather is arguably a better solution. If left uncovered over several seasons, horses will grow a thicker coat, develop a stronger overall constitution to suit their environment, and be able to regulate their body temperature better. Using a rug can be helpful in keeping fine horses warm, to keep a riding horse conveniently clean, and to compensate for the natural warmth lost if a horse is clipped.

However, it is also good for them to get covered in mud, at least from time to time. The act of rolling on the ground provides them with a natural massage, drags out dead hair, stimulates new growth, and lays down a covering of mud to keep out cold winds.

A horse has such sensitive skin that it can feel a tiny fly land on it. While we are often encouraged as children to pat a pony, horses prefer to be stroked or, even better, scratched. When you find a favorite place, often along the mane or on the neck, the horse will stretch, lean into the scratch, and, if you are very lucky, may even scratch you too with its teeth. While it can be uncomfortable to be scratched by an enthusiastic horse with big teeth, most owners love it when their horse decides to scratch them back. Mutual grooming is a sign of trust and part of the relaxed "hanging out" behavior that bonds a herd together.

Curly coats

While the winter coats of most breeds grow long, the Bashkir Pony, from the southern foothills of the Urals, is one of several mountain breeds from the Eurasian steppes that develop a curly coat. They flourish in the extreme environment in which they live and where winter temperatures can drop to below -22° F (-30° C). Like many native breeds, they are superbly adapted for such conditions and have grown to be a key element of the local economy and way of life. Hair from the curly coat is combed and woven into blankets and clothes, and the tough little animals are kept by the local populace for milk, meat, "wool," and work as riding, harness, and pack ponies.

The long history of curly coats on the Russian steppes took an unexplained turn when curly-coated horses were found among the Mustang herds of Nevada in the United States. The Sioux and Crow tribes were said to have bred them from around 1800 onward, and they became part of ranching herds toward the end of the century.

When an exceptionally harsh Nevada winter in the 1930s left stock stranded out on the range, curly-coated horses were the only ones to survive. From then on, they were bred for their resilience, temperament, and stamina as well as for their unusual characteristics. But no one has discovered the secret of their origin, or if they are related to Bashkir Ponies. Research continues, however, and as genetic testing becomes more and more refined, no doubt the findings will provide answers to this conundrum.

They are known as American Bashkir Curlies or American Curly Horses and come in a wide variety of colors, standing taller than the Eurasian breeds. But they share the thick curls that shed to a slightly rippled summer coat, as well as a dense double mane, which falls to both sides of the neck. The mane, tail, the fur inside the ears, and even the eyelashes may also be wavy. The degree of curl varies between individual horses from very tight curls through to slight waves. Some are called "extremes" because of the exceptional nature of their curliness, and some shed out their manes and tails almost completely every year. They grow back the following year. They all share the even more unusual characteristic of being hypoallergenic, which means that their curly coats do not trigger allergies in humans.

View of the world

Like all prey animals, horses evolved an acute sense of vision so that they can spot predators in time to outrun them. Their large eyes are positioned on the sides of the head. This gives them great peripheral vision, meaning that they can see almost all around them. Even if a predator is lurking in the grass or creeping up obliquely from behind, the horse is well-equipped to see its approach. However, if the predator approaches from a head-on position or from directly behind the horse, it is vulnerable. The lateral position of the eyes creates a blind spot directly in front and behind the horse. The forward-facing blind spot also means that a horse has trouble in seeing you if you stand directly in front of it and cannot see a jump in the final few approach strides. The rear-facing blind spot means that a horse is most vulnerable to a silent approach directly from behind.

This explains why novice riders are always warned to keep clear of the horse's hind legs. This is not because horses are aggressive or dangerous by nature, but because instinct tells them to kick out at a sudden presence or unexpected touch from behind. Those powerful hind legs are the most effective way of scaring off a predator prowling near the hindquarters. However, a relaxed horse is unlikely to kick a person if it is used to being handled and the handler speaks reassuringly or keeps one hand on the horse while moving around. This lets the horse maintain a sense of where that person is in relation to its personal space.

The blind spot in front of the horse only extends to around 3 ft (90 cm), but when a horse is looking forward, the blind spot to the rear stretches away indefinitely and is just a little wider than the horse's body. This can lead a horse to panic if it is startled by an unseen car or an unfamiliar noise—all its senses are telling it that there is danger behind and it needs to get away fast. A horse that is tied up or ridden on a tight rein cannot turn its head and body to get a better look, which explains the agitated behavior that may otherwise seem an excessive reaction.

The size of the horse's eye allows maximum visual information to be taken in at long range or in poor light. Horses move around confidently in the natural darkness outdoors and can also cope well in a dark barn or stable once their eyes have adjusted to the low levels of light. They will blink if a light is switched on and some horses can show discomfort in bright sunlight, especially if they have pale eyes due to their coloring.

A horse's eye sees the world in a different way to ours. The center of the eye has a horizontal, rather than round, pupil. This allows for very acute vision in the near to middle distance, while the outer area detects motion.

Right: *As horses cannot see directly behind them, this horse has turned its head and neck, and swivelled one ear to take in as much information as possible.*

Once the horse senses motion, it will move its head to adjust its focus. Using both monocular and binocular vision, it can see something to one side with a single eye and also focus both eyes together to look at what is ahead. This is another reason why a horse may move its position—having seen something with one eye, it may take a second look with both eyes for a fuller assessment and better depth perception. It may want to touch its nose on an unfamiliar object too—using an additional sense to derive information about its surroundings—or it may refuse to get close to something if it does not feel sure that it is safe.

An anxious horse with its head held high cannot see the ground and so may stumble or trip, especially when being kept on a tight rein by a rider who is also anxious. This can make the horse agitated, causing the rider to hold on even tighter and so raising the level of risk. It always makes sense to allow a horse to look at something alarming and to check out the terrain underfoot. It also helps if the rider looks away from an object that is worrying the horse, as the horse will sense the rider's focus, body position, and overall level of relaxation. If the rider seems unconcerned by the situation, then the horse is more likely to relax too.

A horse can adjust its depth perception by lifting, lowering, or angling its head. This helps it to focus on an object, but can make it move in a way that seems very strange until we understand what it is doing. A horse sometimes arcs its whole body to get a better view of something alongside it, or tips its head to one side. If you prevent this natural movement when riding, you can cause a horse to "spook" or "shy" when it encounters a strange object. Sometimes just by allowing the body adjustment, the rider can help the horse to feel more confident in these alarming situations. Some horses are more easily spooked than others, and poor eyesight may be a factor here, although individual temperament and experience are also important influences.

Opposite: *The natural ability of the horse to run stems from its need to survive, but galloping also seems to be something the horse simply loves to do.*

Designed for speed

Horses have evolved naturally to run, but they have also been selectively bred to run especially fast. Over time, many breeds have been developed with the express purpose of enhancing their speed. These include the American Quarter Horse and the English Thoroughbred.

The Quarter Horse is a very versatile breed, famous as a cow pony and ranch horse, as well as being popular for many ridden disciplines. Developed from the same Iberian base stock as the Mustang crossed with "running horses" of mixed native types that arrived with English settlers in the early seventeenth century, it is elegant and very fast. The name comes from the breed's reputation for impressive speed in quarter-mile races that were run through the plantations (and even the streets) of Virginia. The powerful muscle development of the hindquarters hints at the great capacity for forward thrust, while a compact and stocky body with a refined head adds to the breed's overall practical athleticism. The Quarter Horse can turn its hoof to just about anything and this is why it is still the main working ranch horse today. It is the most popular breed in the United States with the largest breed registry in the world, while many other working breeds are now deemed rare or at risk.

The English Thoroughbred was also developed from the "running horses" of the seventeenth century, but British breeders took their horses in a very different direction. While the Quarter Horse is a short, feisty sprinter, the Thoroughbred is taller and finer in build. It is a long, lean horse bred for races that were originally run over 4 miles (6.4 km) or more, sometimes over fences.

Horse racing has been a popular sport in Britain since the Middle Ages but it became closely linked with the monarchy in the seventeenth century. King Charles II was not only a great follower of the sport, but also competed in races himself. With royal support, interest in breeding racehorses grew, as opposed to simply racing the horses that were available. This remains true today, as the British Royal Family, and the Queen especially, are enthusiastic breeders and owners of racing stock. While the Quarter Horse has Spanish blood in its heritage, the Thoroughbred owes much to the Arabian horse. Spanish and Arabian horses share lineage, so their respective links leading back to the desert breeds are clear. They bring refinement, stamina, speed, and prepotency—the capacity to pass on characteristics—to any breed to which they are introduced. The practice of outcrossing to a Spanish or Arabian horse has helped to improve and develop many breeds.

The **Quarter Horse** is a very **versatile** breed, famous as a **cow pony** and ranch horse...it is **elegant** and very **fast**.

Three Arabian stallions—the Godolphin Arabian, the Darley Arabian, and the Byerley Turk—helped to found the English Thoroughbred. None of them was famed for speed, but they brought their qualities of grace and stamina to the running horses bred from native stock over generations. By the end of the eighteenth century, the "racehorse" was established.

The first Stud Book showing the breeding records for the Thoroughbred was published by James Weatherby in 1791. It was entitled *An Introduction to a General Stud Book*, with Volume One of *The General Stud Book* following in 1808. It has continued to be published in updated form every four years to the present day. A horse can only race in Britain if it is registered with Weatherbys, and it can only be registered with Weatherbys if it is a Thoroughbred. This means that every registered Thoroughbred horse has an ancestry that can be traced back to those three Arabian stallions.

While the English Thoroughbred was developed for the specific purpose of racing, it is also used as a riding horse. Crossed with breeds such as the Irish Draft, it can add refinement to more stocky types, while they bring strength and bone to balance the more delicate Thoroughbred influence.

Opposite: *The massive strength of the Shire does not in any way diminish its capacity for speed and grace. Indeed, the huge thundering hooves of a galloping Shire make its speed seem all the more impressive.*

Size and strength

Alongside speed, strength is one of the most impressive physical characteristics of the horse. While the sheer size of the draft breeds, such as the Shire or the Percheron, has immediate impact, breeds such as the diminutive Shetland Pony also possess enormous strength, which belies their size and appearance.

A Shire horse can pull up to twice its own body weight and stands at an average height of 17.2 hh at the withers. Its deep oblique shoulder and long muscles in the hindquarters, with strong hocks in line beneath, give it huge pulling capacity. Teams of Shire horses were once used to tow loads of coal weighing up to 3 tons. They also pulled plows, wagons, and canal boats as, before the advent of steam engines, draft horses provided most of the motive power for agriculture and industry.

For a time the Shire was seriously threatened by the rise of mechanization, but today it has found a new role in the leisure and heritage business. It has also returned to agriculture in small-scale farming, forestry work, and landscape maintenance as the horse's huge hooves cause less damage to sensitive environments than machinery. The silky hair around the fetlocks (ankles) of a Shire horse and other heavy breeds is called the "feathers" and it helps to protect the feet against bad weather, rain, and mud. Shires

are admired for being calm and gentle, despite their great size, and make an impressive riding horse. Their hooves may cause the earth to resound to their tread, but their temperaments make them safe and responsive mounts.

The Shire is also not the only draft breed to find new work in forestry and other delicate environments. A small stocky cob can tow logs without damaging standing trees in restricted areas, negotiate tight turns and narrow paths.

The Percheron was originally a French breed from La Perche, a district of Normandy in northern France, one of the longest-established horse-breeding centers in the world. It is another of the draft breeds famed for its great strength and also the elegance of its proportions, intelligence, and willing approach to work. The breed stands between 15 and 19 hh and is popular worldwide. It was said to be able to trot for 37 miles (60 km) in a day's work during the nineteenth century, when most of the working horses in France were Percherons.

There are many draft types and their role in agriculture has been maintained in some countries despite the Industrial Revolution. Both the value placed on traditional methods and the cost of moving to a mechanized system has meant they remain crucial to some farmers.

One draft-horse tradition that has both a long history and a thriving modern following

Left: *This Russian heavy draft horse gives a hint of the impact that 300 heavy horses recreating the La Route du Poisson must have.*

is La Route du Poisson—The Fish Run—which commemorates the rush to transport fresh fish from the beaches of Boulogne-sur-Mer to the markets of Paris. The history of this practice stretches back many centuries in France. Launched as an international sporting event in 1991 to help promote another French draft breed, the Boulonnais, La Route du Poisson has become a celebration of the strength and stamina of working-horse breeds with teams from across Europe taking part. More than 300 heavy horses thundering along public roads toward Paris is an impressive sight that attracts around 300,000 spectators a year.

At the other end of the size spectrum, miniatures can be just as appealing and impressive as any large horse. The Shetland Pony is a native breed from the Shetland Islands which lie to the northeast of mainland Scotland. Like many native breeds, the Shetland developed to survive in a harsh environment and severe weather. It lived on a foraging diet along the windswept shorelines of its remote native territory. These conditions are partly responsible for its small size; it is traditionally measured in inches, rather than hands, with the maximum height of the breed standard set at 42 in (107 cm). To crofters working their farms in difficult conditions, this tough little pony was an essential companion for riding, driving, and carrying loads across rough terrain.

Right: *This Shetland Pony and Clydesdale are well matched for color and, proportionately speaking, for strength. They also illustrate the strong friendships that horses of very different types can forge.*

Exceptionally strong in proportion to its size, the Shetland develops a dense coat and long mane, making it resilient to harsh weather, and it has round, strong hooves. It does well on a poor diet—indeed far better than on good grazing that can lead to health problems. It also has a lot of character, being intelligent and quick to learn, and plenty of common sense. Sadly, all these characteristics meant that hundreds of thousands of Shetlands were once used to work underground in mines. Today, they are popular as children's ponies, as well as for driving and showing. In the United States the Shetland Pony has been bred taller than its Scottish cousins. There are also Miniature Shetlands, which are often smaller than a large dog, but they all still retain the vitality and character of the breed.

The Caspian, a rare breed originally from Iran, is similar in size to a standard Shetland Pony, but is significantly different in character. Caspians are classed as horses, not ponies, due to their physical characteristics and action. They move with a long, low action and have elegant proportions. Known for strength and an exceptional jumping ability, as well as a kind and willing temperament, they are thought to descend from strong, fast, and agile horses bred in Persia to pull chariots as long ago as 3400 BC.

Exceptionally strong in proportion to its size, the **Shetland Pony**…has a lot of **character**, being **intelligent** and quick to learn, with plenty of **common sense**.

Hoof health

People who care for horses understand how important it is to look after their welfare. It takes long training and years of study to become a vet, saddler, farrier, trainer, or horse psychologist, and this dedication shows that people realize that horse ownership is a responsibility that must be taken seriously. Whether a prize-winning racehorse or a family pony, the basic physical needs of the horse remain the same and require knowledge and dedication from all owners.

Among the most challenging physical needs of the horse is hoof soundness. The old saying, "no hoof, no horse," is quite true. The horse's hoof is a very complex part of its anatomy and while horses can successfully travel hundreds of kilometres, shod or unshod (*see* above), without harm, a hoof abscess or a bruised sole may halt

them for weeks. As hooves are also affected by digestion and metabolism, the health of the whole horse is reflected in the condition of its hoof.

It is made of the same sort of material as animal horn or human nails, with an outer wall—the hoof capsule—which provides a tough shield to protect the delicate inner workings of the foot. The way the hoof functions when it comes into contact with the ground is known as the "hoof mechanism." This mechanism determines the way the blood is pumped around the hoof to and from the leg and is linked to the speed of movement and the position of the hoof on and off the ground. The detailed physiology of this is very complicated, but at the most simple level suffice it to say that the hoof is not a solid block—it contracts and expands as the horse moves, and can get stronger or weaker depending on how the

horse is kept, the type of ground over which it has to move, and its diet.

The American Mustang is often held up as an example as it shows the toughness, movement, and adaptability of the natural hoof in difficult terrain—these horses receive no special human care or attention. They live or die by the health of their hooves because a damaged hoof will severely impair movement—lame horses are unable to keep up with the herd, or escape from danger, or forage widely for food. Horses in wetter climates face different challenges as it is important for the hoof to be regularly exposed to both wet and dry ground, and horses that are stabled or live in muddy conditions may have difficulty maintaining strong hooves.

One of the most interesting aspects of the hoof is the "frog," a soft V-shaped wedge that supports the underside of the foot and forms a bridge between the two outer edges of the hoof. As the horse moves, the hoof expands and contracts, and the frog cushions the movement, giving spring and protecting the leg above from the shock of impact.

While shoeing horses is a traditional practice, today the interest in keeping horses barefoot, using a specialized trim to imitate natural wear, is growing steadily. Once more, the Mustang provides the example of how strong and healthy an unshod hoof can be. It is no longer unusual to see barefoot horses participating in many competitive disciplines over all terrains, as well as in more leisurely or working activities. All 38 horses of the Houston Police Mounted Patrol in Texas have been barefoot since 2003; this is a striking testimony to a new approach to keeping horses that have to be at peak fitness whenever they are needed.

The physiology of the horse is a vast and fascinating subject. A full understanding of the workings of all its muscles, nerves, and skeletal structure demands years of study, but even if we only watch horses grazing as we pass by in a car or on the way to work, knowing a little of what is going on under the skin offers a new insight into their lives. All their senses are alert to the slightest movement, sound, smell, or touch. Their posture, attitude, and subtle movements send signals to the horses around them. They are never doing nothing—even when they are doing nothing.

Left: *This Andalusian stallion sums up the physical attributes of all horses in his obvious power and strength, the alertness of his posture and expression, and the grace of his overall form.*

Colors and markings

Beautiful coats of many colors

> **❝** At first glance, the herd seems to be similar in color—fall shades of russet and brown. But as we look closer, we can see that some have black manes and tails while others have manes that are more golden than their horse chestnut-colored coats. One mealy-colored mare has a black strip that runs the length of her spine and markings like zebra stripes on her legs. And hidden in their midst, two of the foals are patched all over, one black and white and one a golden-brown and white. As the little black and white one turns to cast a curious glance at us, we see that his eyes are blue. **❞**

There's an old saying that a good horse is never a bad color and there are certainly plenty of colors from which to choose. There are fashions in horse colors as in anything else, as humans tend to be drawn to color, so it's not unusual for people to have a favorite. Perhaps more surprisingly, horses show color preference too, especially stallions when choosing a mate. This is well-documented behavior and Charles Darwin, pioneer of the theory of evolution, noted in the nineteenth century that semiwild horses tended to select mates that were similar in color to themselves.

More recently, researchers observing wild Mustang herds in Montana and Nevada observed that some stallions gathered mares of a single color. It is hard to tell, however, if this is a preference based on appearance, or a more subtle instinctive recognition of genetic background. Theories on the way horses perceive the world suggest that the color of a stallion's mother or immediate herd-members may also influence this preference. In that case, the choice of color would not necessarily signify preference or even instinct, but rather the familiarity that creates a sense of safety, which is always important to horses. As not all stallions exhibit this color-preference trait and domestic horses breed successfully though they are rarely given a choice of mate, the personality of the individual must also play a part.

For domestic horses, color preferences are often governed by fashion. For instance, over the past 20 or 30 years, colored horses (those with broken colors such as black or brown with white)

have become very popular. Before then, mixed colors were seen as evidence of unknown breeding and so they were distinctly unpopular. Color choice can also reflect what is simply practical at a certain point in history. In the days when the horse and carriage was the prevalent mode of transport, a smart matched pair of bays, chestnuts, or grays were relatively easy to find, and they suited the conservative tastes of wealthy owners or businessmen.

Color has also always been very important to breed standards that aim to preserve the defining traits and characteristics of individual breeds. This is especially vital in a breed that is at risk, such as the Cleveland Bay, which is always bay with a black mane and tail, or the Suffolk Punch, which is always chestnut. As well as the familiar solid colors, horses are found with spots, patches, and even a few stripes. But not all black horses are truly black and there has also long been debate over what exactly makes a horse "white." Those with dorsal stripes and zebra markings on their legs are often described as having "primitive" characteristics and a horse with spots can turn up occasionally, even in breeds that are not usually spotty.

The genetic patterns that lead to all these colors are complex, and knowing the breed history can help breeders predict—or plan—the color of an unborn foal. While some colors may be seen as more desirable than others, color also provides information about genetic makeup. This can be important to someone aiming to breed for a specific purpose. However, nature is hard to predict with exactitude and anyone breeding for a particular color should expect a few surprises, which is probably a good thing.

Some breeds are always variations on the same color. For instance, the pretty Austrian Haflinger

(see above) is chestnut, ranging from pale to dark, with a flaxen mane and tail. The majestic Netherlands horse—the Friesian—is always black today, although this was not the case in the past when gray and chestnut were also seen. But the modern breed standard, developed to help the breed survive when it became very rare in the early twentieth century, requires that all registered horses have to be black and the only white permitted is a small star on the forehead. A typical gray Arabian, sorrel Quarter Horse, and bay English Thoroughbred are well-loved classic colors, but many other colors are found in all three breeds.

" The **majestic** Netherlands horse—the **Friesian**—is **always black** today, although this was not the case in the past when **gray and chestnut** were also seen. "

Right: *Black and white? Or dark bay and gray? Horse colors are not always what they seem. Sunlight reflected on a black coat might suggest the horse on the left is bay, but gray knees and dark eyes prove the horse on the right is gray.*

Genetic color code

Color is determined by the genes provided by each parent, which are always in pairs but are not equal. One is always dominant and one always recessive, which means that the traits of the dominant gene will always be stronger than the traits of the recessive one. This is not related to the gender of the parent but to the breeding of each one and when those genes are matching, they will pass along the same color characteristics. Gray is dominant over all other colors, while chestnut is always recessive. This means that a horse with one gray parent will become gray, even if it is not born gray, and irrespective of what color the other parent is.

But a horse is less likely to be chestnut than any other color unless both parents are chestnut, when the likelihood of a chestnut foal is very high. The terms "chestnut" and "sorrel" are often used interchangeably, and both mean a reddish-brown, though "sorrel" can sometimes be used specifically to mean a copper-colored chestnut. These terms also depend on geography—in the U.K., the term "sorrel" is unusual for any sort of chestnut horse, while it is very common in the United States.

The base pigment of all horse colors is either red or black, with black also including bay, as they stem from the same dominant gene. From that starting point, the variations in color come from

Opposite: *This dappled gray may well have started life as a very dark foal and become gradually paler with each passing year of maturity.*

dilutions, patterns, and modifiers that influence the base pigments. This variation might be visible over the whole body or only on what we call the points, which are the mane, tail, lower legs, and around the ears. There are around ten other genes that modify these to create the range of colors we see in horses. These are known as "dilutions" and there are at least five possible dilutions to the base pigments. These are silver, champagne, cream, dun, and pearl and the amount of each dilution, and whether it is dominant or recessive, will influence the coat color.

If a horse is homozygous, this means it carries two identical copies of the gene that provides a certain trait—therefore, that trait will appear in its offspring. For a recessive gene to be passed on, the matching pair must be recessive. If it is heterozygous, it does not have matching genes, so its offspring will carry the dominant traits.

While gray is always dominant over other colors, it is not actually a true color, as it derives from a modifier gene that replaces dark hairs with light ones over time. True gray horses have dark skin and dark eyes, and are usually born bay or chestnut, or black. Even horses that are born very dark gray will lighten over the years. This is not necessarily a sign of old age, as they may change from dark to light even before they are fully grown. A foal that is born dark may start to turn gray as it

sheds its initial soft baby coat at around four to six months old. A first sign of the lighter color is often the appearance of gray "goggles" around the eyes. The lightening process is related to the growth of the winter and summer coats, so more light hairs appear each year while darker ones are shed.

Lipizzaners, famous as the white horses of the Spanish Riding School of Vienna, are an especially good example of the changing tones of the gray. They are always born bay or black but will have turned varying shades of gray by the time they are between six and ten years old.

Gray horses may have a dark mane and tail, though these may lighten too, depending on the breed. A flea-bitten gray (one flecked with darker-colored hairs) usually starts as very dark and then lightens to very pale with specks of reddish-brown all over. Interestingly, the flecks often increase as the horse gets older and, in rare examples, become so dense that it appears to have reverted to a solid color.

A dappled gray has distinctive lighter rings of gray, sometimes more profusely on the rump and shoulders, and often retains a darker mane and tail. A rose gray is a delicate color with a slight pinkish tint from red hairs in the coat. While particularly associated with Arabian horses, rose gray shows up in other breeds too. Any horse with the gray gene that is born bay or chestnut could become a rose

Right: *This elegant Lipizzaner will have been born very dark brown or black, but gradually changed to this "white-gray" before reaching ten years of age.*

gray, but as the degree of "rosiness" varies from horse to horse, some never go through this phase.

A steel gray is very striking—it has a dark coat with a silvery color deriving from a black base coat mixed with lighter gray hair. Steel grays rarely stay this color for long and often turn flea-bitten or dappled as time passes.

Variations on a theme

While gray horses can become "white," strictly speaking they are always gray if they have the dark eyes and skin that shows the gray gene. Other colors can go white over time, but they are not born white. Some experts consider that true white horses must be born white and have one white parent. This theory argues that there is a dominant white gene. However, as white horses are occasionally born to parents of other colors, this is debatable and there remains a great deal of disagreement about color patterns, particularly the more unusual ones. As this can be very important to horse-breeders, genetic testing is now often carried out to determine a true color. The defining features of any white horse are a truly white coat from birth and also pink skin and brown eyes, though occasionally blue eyes turn up.

Cremello horses are sometimes called "white" or "albino" but neither description is accurate as a cremello horse has two cream genes resulting

> A **flea-bitten gray**…usually starts as very dark and then **lightens** to very pale with **specks of reddish-brown** all over.

Right: *This striking horse is a perlino, a color resultant from two cream genes. The slightly darker cream of his mane distinguishes him from a cremello, which would have a white mane and tail.*

in a cream-colored coat. This is called "double dilution." The difference from white is very noticeable in a cremello that also has white markings on its creamy coat.

The champagne-colored horse can come in many variations of pale gold. It has bright blue eyes at birth that slowly change to light hazel, and very pink skin that freckles with age. A horse with one champagne gene will always be champagne, with the color variation being determined by the recessive gene. The colors include "gold" (champagne and chestnut), and "classic" (champagne and black). They are largely associated with particular breeds: Quarter Horses, Tennessee Walking Horses, Missouri Fox Trotters, and American Saddlebreds all show this coloring.

Horses of various different colors may be described as "roans," though roan is not a color itself. A roan is a horse of a solid color with single white hairs, rather than spots or patches, across the body. The roan gene simply adds white hairs and can show up in any color. Some of the most common are red or strawberry roan, blue roan, gray roan, bay roan, and dun roans. The points are usually darker than the body and roans do not lose their base color with age in the way that a gray does.

Many solid colors, such as bay, chestnut, and dun, also remain constant throughout a horse's life. They may vary in depth between horses and

Opposite: Pure gold—the lovely palomino coloring adds a fairy-tale quality to many breeds. A palomino may range from pale to dark, but it always has a blonde mane and tail.

be bleached paler by the sun, but they will not change significantly over time.

Palominos also usually keep their color—a glossy gold beautifully highlighted by a light blonde or cream-colored mane and tail. Palominos can be various gold shades and, depending on their breeding, may have darker dapples, known as "soot marks," which occur in other light colors too. Palominos are very easy to recognize and many breeds may have palomino coloring, usually with dark eyes and skin. While pale chestnuts or darker cremellos may sometimes look very like a palomino, it is the genetic make-up that determines the color, not the appearance. While the palomino is not a breed, there are many color registries to promote them and they are always popular: the combination of the rich gold coat and blonde mane gives them a magical fairy-tale quality. Interestingly, registered Thoroughbred and Arabian horses may be any solid color except palomino.

Historically, palominos were (and often still are) known as "Isabellas," in tribute to Queen Isabella of Spain, who in the fifteenth century famously sponsored the voyages of Christopher Columbus to the New World. She was said to have kept 100 gold horses and to have sent a stallion and mares to the New World, thereby introducing the color to the Americas.

Black is another very striking solid color but, like white, is not always what it seems. A true black horse is quite unusual, except in breeds defined by the color, such as Fell and Dales Ponies and the Friesian. Both Fell and Dales Ponies are predominantly black, and certain similarities of shape and carriage with the Friesian, as well as the color, hint at historic links between the breeds.

While a dark bay or liver chestnut can sometimes appear to be black, a black horse will have no other colors at all—no hints of red or roaning, for instance—and will have black, rather than dark, skin and dark eyes. While gray foals are often born black, black foals are more often a mousy color, and may have leg stripes. While this can result in them being mistaken for other colors, the stripes will fade as the foal grows and turns true black. Black coats can fade in the sun, which can cause confusion, but those that do not are known as "sheer blacks." There are also horses that are classified as black because of their breeding, but which appear chocolate brown in color. What you see is frequently not what you get with horse colors.

This can cause controversy because perception of color can be very much in the eye of the beholder. This may seem of little significance to the casual observer, but it is vital to a breeder or serious enthusiast who will use genetic testing to help define color. This knowledge can then be used to

Left: *These attractive Konik ponies are a very good example of blue dun coloring and the so-called "primitive" markings, especially the black dorsal stripe, indicative of a very ancient heritage.*

determine future breeding efforts in which color or specific physical features are important.

Gray as a crane

One of the most debated colors is the *grulla* or *grullo*, also known as the silver dun, blue dun, black dun, silver *grulla*, smoky *grulla*, mouse dun and gray dun. The names that aim to describe the color seem endless and vary from breed to breed, with names like lilac dun, lobo dun, olive dun, black buckskin, slate, and chocolate illustrating the difficulty of defining the different shades.

The term *grullo* tends to be used for American breeds and is usually accepted to come from the Spanish for "crane," because this bird is a similar smoky gray and black color. In this case, a *grullo* is a male horse and a *grulla* is a female. But both terms are frequently used without reference to gender—they are pronounced "grew-ya" or "grew-yo." European breeds of this color tend to be defined as silver duns.

As the color ranges from a silvery blue to a chocolate brown or even black, it is unsurprising that it is difficult to agree on what to call it. But it does have some defining features and, genetically speaking, it is a black horse with at least one dominant dun-factor gene. This dilutes the black base pigment and adds dun factor features to the horse's body.

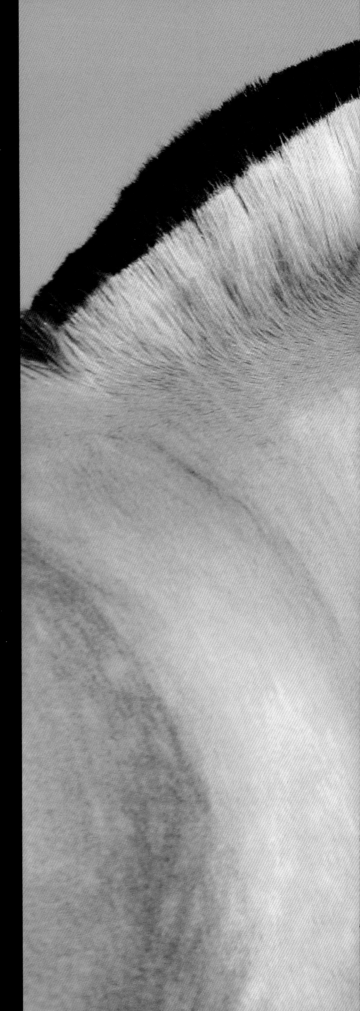

Dun features are very distinctive and a horse may have some or all of them. However, the one defining feature is a dorsal stripe running the length of the spine from ears to tail. While it is often lost in the mane and tail hair, it will show up in a horse with a lighter colored mane and tail, such as the Norwegian Fjord Horse. This breed is always shades of dun and has a very distinctive blonde mane with the black stripe clearly visible through the center, though the depth of color may vary from horse to horse. It is traditional to trim the mane of the Norwegian Fjord so that it stands up in a crescent to accentuate this attractive feature. Duns often have horizontal stripes on the legs, known as "primitive markings" or "zebra stripes"—this feature is often seen in the Fjord. Highland Ponies, native to Scotland, also display a full range of dun colorings, though they may also be black, gray, and brown.

Right: *This distinctive style of mane trim, traditional for the Norwegian Fjord, shows off the dark dorsal stripe running through the pale mane as a striking feature.*

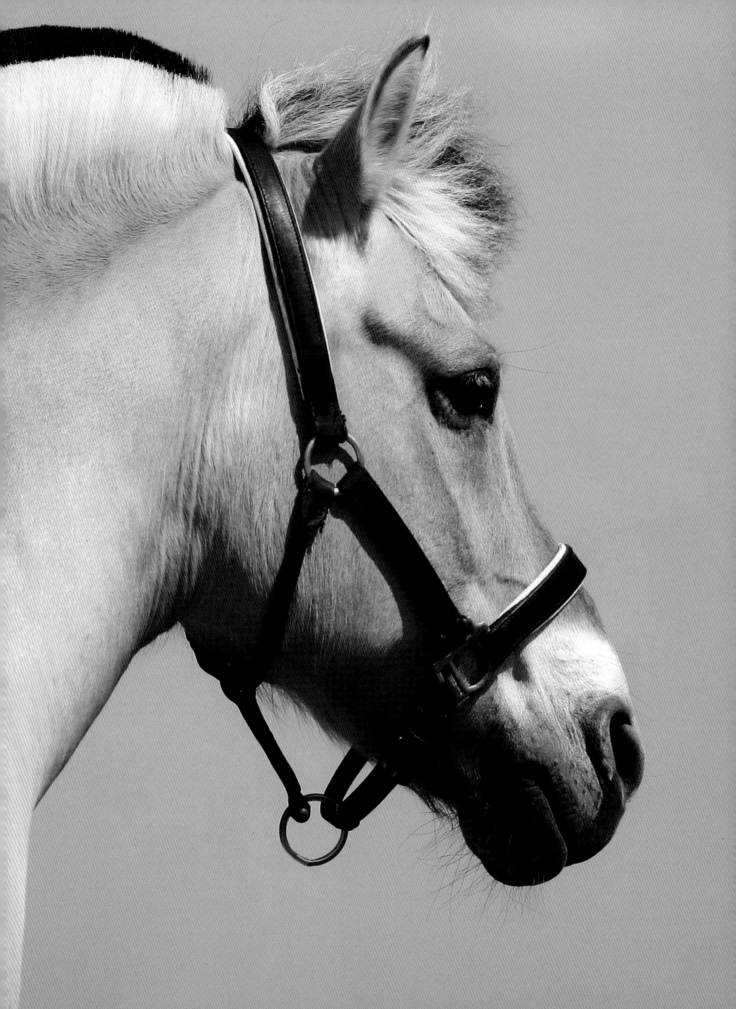

Duns come in several color variations. A *grulla* or silver dun combines a dorsal stripe with a coat that has a smoky, mouse-colored or chocolate tint. This is quite a rare color, yet it occurs in several breeds, including the Quarter Horse, Appaloosa, Highland Pony, Icelandic Horse, and Shetland Pony. Breed and color registries continue to argue about the definition of the color, but the black mane and tail and dorsal stripe with black on the lower legs are generally accepted features.

The *grulla* has a dark pigmented skin, well adapted to withstand sunlight, yet it occurs in many cold-weather breeds. The coat can also change with the seasons, with the dark mane developing chestnut tinges during a bright summer. While it is usually a solid color, a *grulla* Appaloosa is very likely to have at least some white hairs in its coat.

The Icelandic Horse is an interesting example of a breed that displays an exceptionally wide range of colors. It has been deliberately pure-bred for more than 800 years and, with no influence of cross-breeding, remains very true to type. A defining feature of its native country, these small, tough horses are, even today, vital to the lives of people who live in a landscape that is still more easily crossed on horseback than by any other means. Distinguished by size, strength and its unique pace—the smooth four-beat running walk known as *tölt*—the Icelandic Horse is found in 100 variations of 40 different colors. One of several types of the dun is the silver dun; the misty color and dark points blend beautifully with Iceland's dramatic landscape.

The Palouse horse

One of the most colorful and loudly patterned breeds is the spotted Appaloosa. Bred by the Nez Percé tribe of the Palouse region in what is now the northwest of the United States, they were distinguished by their colored coats, their stamina, and temperament. The breed was persecuted almost to extinction during the nineteenth century by the U.S. Government's attempts to control the Nez Percé tribespeople. They survive today due to a small number of dedicated breeders who sought out the few remaining horses to build the breed up to strength once more. The Appaloosa Horse Club was formed in 1938 and today there are more than 600,000 registered horses.

As well as their spotted coats, Appaloosas also have striped hooves and mottled pink and dark skin all over their body. While this is most noticeable around the muzzle and eyes, it may also be seen under the coat if the horse is wet. Interestingly, the patterns on the skin do not always match the spots on the coat, but they remain consistent even if the coat changes.

Distinguished by size, **strength**, and its unique pace—the smooth four-beat **running walk** known as *tölt*—the **Icelandic Horse** is found in 100 variations of **40 different colors.**

Right: *This blanket-spot Appaloosa has "varnish marks" around its black and brown spots, and shows signs of "roaning out" in the white hairs across its body. Its coat may become paler over a number of years.*

The basic coat patterns are blanket spot, leopard spot, few spot, and snowflake. Each one describes a specific pattern, although all have many variations. A blanket spot is a horse that is largely a solid color but has a white patch on its hindquarters spotted with the main body color. A blanket spot pattern often "roans out," meaning that the amount of white in the coat increases over the years and may in time cover the whole body.

A leopard spot is a horse that has a white or cream base coat with varying degrees of spots of black, brown, or chestnut color (and sometimes all three) over its body. The spots may have a shadowy mark around them. These are called "varnish marks" and they tend to remain fairly consistent. Hard-edged spots tend to fade over time but, with an Appaloosa, very little is certain when it comes to the effects of age on coat color and markings.

A few spot is a pale body with a small number of spots—sometimes even just one—while a snowflake is a dark color with white spots that often look more like flecks in appearance. An Appaloosa may also be a solid color, though this could roan out as it gets older.

Appaloosas may also have a thin mane and tail, which is sometimes so sparse it is called a "rat-tail," and a ring around the iris of the eye (or sclera), which is present but not visible in other breeds.

Left: *Spotted horses are striking but can also be well camouflaged—this leopard spot would blend as well into the trees in the background as his white-gray companion does into the snow.*

The Danish Knabstrup is another famous spotted breed, bred in Denmark since the seventeenth century. With Spanish ancestry, these stunning horses were reserved for royalty and nobility. Like the Appaloosa, they display varying numbers of spots, and few-spot horses—known as "white born"—were used as carriage horses. They also distinguished themselves in the riding academy of the Danish court in the early days of classical riding, their appearance adding impressive presence to show off the skills of horse and rider. Sadly, the royal breeding line lost its original color over time, possibly due to the presence of a gray gene.

There are other spotted breeds and types, including the Tiger Horse, a breed that has only been in development since 1992. Looking to reach back to the Spanish ancestry of the spotted horses imported into the United States in the sixteenth century and to even earlier ancestral roots, the Tiger Horse Association holds up the seventh-century Soulon leopard-spotted horse of China as its ideal. Tiger Horses are always gaited, which means they display lateral and "running walk" paces naturally; a defining feature alongside their Appaloosa coloring.

Opposite: *This unusual Appaloosa coloring may roan out completely over the passage of several years, leaving a horse that is a creamy color.*

Above: *The American Paint Horse is very popular in Western competition as a versatile all-round horse. It is athletic and quick to learn, with a striking appearance.*

Spots and patches

The Pony of the Americas is a completely new breed, dating from the early 1950s. It was developed to produce a child's pony with Appaloosa coloring but with the smaller proportions of the Shetland Pony. In both cases, understanding the genetic background that determined not only the coat color, but also size and gait, meant that breeders could focus on reproducing the desired features.

"The **Pony of the Americas**…is a child's pony with **Appaloosa coloring** and the smaller **proportions** of the Shetland Pony. "

Horses with patches of color on a white coat or patches of white on a colored coat are more familiar than spotted horses, and they come in all shapes and sizes. The variations do not only refer to the horses themselves but also to the collection of terms used to describe them. For example, in Great Britain, the terms "colored," "piebald," and "skewbald" are used to describe these patterns, whereas "pinto" and "paint" are terms more commonly used in the United States.

The word "pie" or "pi" is a very old one. It means having patches of more than one color, with the emphasis on black and white like a magpie. "Skew" is also a word of ancient origin, while "bald" is simply an old word for "white." "Pinto" comes from a Spanish word meaning "painted," while "paint," of course, simply refers to the painted appearance of these colorful horses.

A piebald horse has large patches of black and white, which usually take the form of black patches on a white base coat. A skewbald is any solid color or colors (other than black) with white patches, or it may be mainly white with colored patches. So skewbalds may have, for example, gray, chestnut, bay, or palomino patches, and are sometimes described as blue and white, red and white, or lemon and white. They may have some black markings too, but these will be insignificant in relation to the main coat color.

While the terms "pinto" and "paint" may be used for both piebald and skewbald horses, there can be very significant differences if the terms are associated with particular breeds or color registries. While the Pinto Horse Association of America is a color registry open to many breeds, under certain specific rules, the American Paint Horse is a breed in its own right, developed from specific bloodlines for color and the features of the athletic and quick-witted working stock horse.

Within the specialized vocabulary relating to colors, the terms "tobiano" and "overo" are in common use. Both tobiano and overo coat patterns appear in horses and ponies of various sizes, breeds and types. A tobiano is generally a white horse with large, irregular, but clearly outlined, patches of solid color across its body. It frequently has white legs below the knee, solid coloring on the face, and the tail may be two colors. An overo, however, is generally a solid color with white on either side of its body in patches, rarely crossing the back. The white markings are often splashes or ragged shapes. The overo has a solid colored tail and distinctive head markings. Where white extends over the eyes and ears, this is called a "bonnet face." If this starts between the eyes and extends around the muzzle, then it is called an "apron face." When much of the whole area is white, it is called a "bald face," linking to the old word for white once more.

"Skewbalds may have…gray, **chestnut**, bay, or palomino **patches** and are sometimes described as blue and white, **red and white**, or lemon and white.**"**

Left: *The Gypsy Vanner combines strength and character with a stocky build and distinctive coloring to make an attractive horse that can be ridden or driven.*

Along with distinctive facial markings like the apron face or bald face, there are also terms that describe more unusual markings. The "medicine hat" is a horse with dark coloring around the ears while the rest of its head is white. Today, there is a Medicine Hat Horse Association, but at one time these horses were so rare that they were considered magical, the mount of choice for a shaman or medicine man. Also known as a "war bonnet," the Native American Plains tribes believed that such horses protected the rider in battle and could warn them of approaching danger. A medicine hat horse with blue eyes was especially prized as being a creature that could cross the boundaries between the earthly and heavenly plains.

Piebald and skewbald horses have a long association with Romany people, Travelers, or Gypsies, whose love of all that is flamboyant extends to their choice of horses. While there are many types and breeds of colored horse, one of the most striking is the Gypsy Vanner or Gypsy Cob. These small draft or cob types were originally bred to pull caravans. They needed to be strong, trainable good-doers both for a life on the road and also to advertise the famous "Gypsy skill" with horses at horse-fairs and markets.

Today, the Gypsy Vanner is established as a breed based on physical characteristics and bloodlines, not simply on color. However, the most

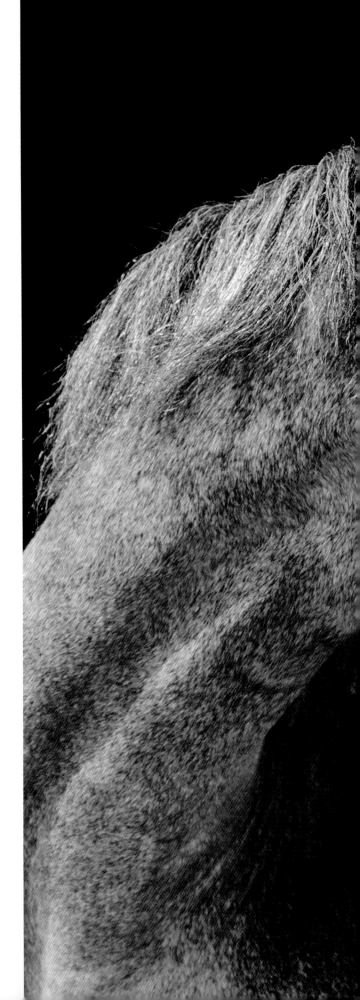

Right: *This horse may be described as a rose gray or a gray roan, as it has a strong tinge of chestnut or bay, even though it is clearly a gray and will become lighter as it gets older.*

admired markings are piebald and skewbald—all other colors are classified as "odd." Among the strong tobiano markings, an overo type known by the Gypsy term "blagdon" is a strong feature of the breed, where a solid color has splashes of white or roaning around the belly and often a bald face.

Many horse colors have names that seek to describe them, often in rather poetic terms. The lobo dun, discussed above, refers to the color of a timber wolf (*lobo* means wolf in Spanish), while describing a horse as "blue" or "rose" tries to suggest a particular shade of gray. Even colors like bay and chestnut vary from horse to horse and from season to season.

More common markings are shared by many breeds and types. Among the most common, and perhaps the best loved, is a white "star" in the very center of the forehead. It can be big or small as long as it is centered on the whorl of hairs in the middle of the face. If a white marking covers or partly covers the center of the face, it is called a "blaze"—this is also very common. A narrow line down the face is called a "stripe." A "snip" is a small white line on the muzzle, often combined with a glimpse of pink skin. Stars, blazes, stripes, and snips may be found in various combinations and have no particular significance except to add to the overall appeal of a particular face.

Left: *The Rocky Mountain Horse has a distinctive range of unusual colors, but this chocolate hue with a flaxen mane and tail is something of a breed trademark.*

Science and superstition

Beliefs and superstitions that associate a horse's color or markings with its temperament or abilities are still widely held today. The long tradition that white or striped hooves are weak flies in the face of modern knowledge that they are no different to dark hooves. Similarly, horses with a "wall" or blue eye, while prized among Native American tribes and Gypsies, may also be treated with suspicion as potentially unreliable or bad tempered.

While most horses have brown eyes, blue eyes are not uncommon, especially in cremellos and other pale coat colors. Horses with patterned coats, such as paints, coloreds or Appaloosas, may also have blue or part-colored blue and brown eyes. The blue color is in the iris and, while horses with light-colored eyes may be more sensitive to bright sunlight, blue irises are just as healthy as brown ones. They have no bearing at all on temperament.

There are many other unusual and striking colors, often found rarely or only in certain breeds. The silver dapple is a color particularly associated with the Rocky Mountain Horse and is a wonderful rich chocolate or gold color with a silver-sheened mane and tail. It may also be called a chocolate, taffy, or flax dapple.

The shiny, metallic gleam of the coat of the Akhal-Teke, a breed originally from Turkmenistan, ed to its nickname of the "Golden Horse," although it comes in many different colors.

The complex genetics behind all the different colors and coat patterns can be very confusing, especially as experts don't always agree and the sophistication of genetic testing is continually refined. For the average owner or enthusiast, breeding for color may seem manipulative and unnatural, yet in many cases the intervention of careful breeding programs have saved breeds that would otherwise have been lost. Yet, at a far deeper level, the natural colors of the horse and its decorative spots and stripes, bring to mind an ancient past and recall life on Earth as revealed in cave paintings from prehistoric times. The horses of today, no matter what their breed or color, have roots that stretch intriguingly into the past.

Right: *The Akhal-Teke is always highly prized not only for its graceful appearance and polished colors, but also for its great intelligence and kind nature.*

Young horses
Growth and development

> As the sun begins to set, the lazy summer herd stirs from dozing and a few horses wander out of their close grouping to graze. In a sudden burst of movement, two leggy half-grown youngsters dart away, chasing each other in sweeping circles around the group. They rear on their hind legs, play-boxing and nipping each other before breaking apart. They snort and buck, then speed away, tails streaming out behind them and heads held high. The older horses ignore them, but the foals are excited and cavort around their mothers. Not bold enough to stray far, they dart about in the golden light of dusk, then scoot back to suckle.

Foals are among the most attractive of young animals, with their gangly legs and soft whiskers. They are often seen peeping around their mothers' flanks, or boldly wandering off to explore and then careering back to safety. A horse is not thought to be an adult until it is around five years old and it has a long journey to make to maturity over that time. The upbringing of a wild foal is very different from that of a domestic foal but, for both of them, interaction with other horses, humans, and the world around them will shape their confidence and behavior for the rest of their lives.

A mare is pregnant for 11 months and the breeding cycle of horses means that foals tend to be born in the spring or early summer. While this happens naturally in the wild, domestic breeders also tend to plan for spring foals. A spring birth provides the mare with the best grass to produce her milk while the foal can enjoy good grazing and the warm weather of summer to grow strong. Horses sometimes give birth to twins, but it is quite rare for both to survive because a mare's body has not evolved to carry two foals to full term.

As prey animals, horses must always be ready to be on the move, so the first instinct of a mare once her foal is born is to urge it onto its feet. She will lick the foal clean, which encourages blood circulation, while nuzzling and nudging it until it attempts to stand. This may take several falls and false starts to achieve, but the long legs that initially seem to be an impediment will soon start to support the foal. A healthy foal will be on its feet very shortly after birth and ready to run from danger within an hour or so.

Opposite: *A foal is strong enough to run alongside its mother when only a few hours old. This is essential to improve chances of survival in the wild.*

To provide strength and to stabilize and stimulate its system, the first requirement is mother's milk. In the hours before and after birth, the mare will produce the especially nutrient-rich milk—colostrum—in the same way as a human mother does. This is easy to digest and full of the antibodies the foal needs to survive until its own immune system can provide protection. It is vital for the foal to have this special milk. If it does not get it, the foal will be far more vulnerable in the early weeks of its life. It is possible to get a colostrum replacer for a foal whose mother cannot feed it, but nothing is as good as this first milk produced by the mother.

The bonding between mother and foal also takes places during this time when it is learning to stand and taking its first feed. The foal will become imprinted upon her, which means it will follow her lead, know her scent, and trust her in a way that will be vital to its survival while it is small. She too will know the foal from all others and develop her maternal feelings of protectiveness. A mare can become very aggressive toward anyone who attempts to touch her foal and will attack a predator without hesitation. Mares in a wild herd will often defend the foals of other mares too, and sometimes a mare whose foal dies may try to steal a foal from another mare. Mares show grief if they lose a foal and the mothering instinct means that a mare will cross all barriers, no matter how dangerous, to reach her foal.

For domestic breeders, organizations called "foaling banks" help owners to connect orphaned foals with mares whose foals have died. A successful adoption is a delicate process as the bereaved mare needs to accept the orphaned foal as her own. This is usually achieved by making sure that her scent and the scent of her own foal mask the scent of the orphan until she has accepted it. It may be several days before it is entirely safe to leave them alone together, as a confused and distressed mare may attack—and even kill—a substitute foal. Once she has accepted the newcomer, however, she will protect it with her life.

Even a mare who is a well-loved family member can become so protective of her offspring that she will not let her usual handlers come near her foal. This anxiety usually dissipates over time. Most owners attempt to handle the foal in the first few days and to make sure that the mare is comfortable with that. This not only helps with handling when the foal is bigger and stronger, but also means that any health problems or visits from the vet are more easily dealt with. The imprinting process can be deliberately extended to include humans by a routine of handling the foal over the first few days and weeks of its life. This includes touching it all over, especially around the head and girth

Right: *Exmoor ponies are a "free-living" breed that run in semiwild herds. Their foals are born out on the open moor and are not handled by humans until they are rounded up when they are old enough to wean.*

areas, and handling its feet. The idea is that having been used to this from birth, the foal will accept haltering, grooming, and other handling far more readily later on. This is a controversial system, however, as it does involve intruding upon those first hours when a mare and foal are getting to know one another. It can also result in a foal that is too confident with humans. This may be very cute when it is tiny, but a foal that jumps up to put its hooves on someone's shoulders is less appealing by the time it's a year old!

Allowing the mare and foal to bond without interference and then introducing handling in a relaxed way is an alternative strategy that is worth the extra patience it requires. As with most methods of horse handling, a quiet, unobtrusive approach may take a little longer, but it will usually have good results.

Quite often a mare and foal will be isolated in a domestic situation, either put into a separate field or paddock away from other horses, or in a large stable called a "foaling box." The mare needs room as she prepares to give birth as she will pace about, walk in circles, lie down and get up again many times. She may foal standing up or lying down and is more likely to do so during the night. Once the foal is born, it is best to leave the two alone together for a while. This affords them some peace from the attention of other horses, who may be

over-curious. However, the sooner the pair return to the company of any horses with which they will be living the better, as horses are generally very tolerant and gentle with young foals.

Nature's way

The advantage of an outdoor birth is that infection is less likely to occur in a clean field. However, the advantage of a stable is that it provides protection from the elements and it is easier to keep an eye on things, either by regular checking or using CCTV. Most mares foal without any complications, but if a vet should be needed, the fact that the horses are under cover and in good light might save two lives. A first-time mother is sometimes afraid and may reject her foal so a sensible handler nearby can reassure her and help the pair to settle. However, some mares will deliberately hold the foal back until their human watchers have decided that nothing is happening and gone to bed. Keeping a quiet watch from a discreet distance is the best course in most cases. You are not interfering but are ready to help or call a vet if necessary.

The instinct to foal alone and in darkness is very strong, and in the wild the mare will go off on her own to give birth. This, of course, makes her vulnerable to predators both during and immediately after the birth, and she will attempt to rejoin the herd as soon as possible.

The **foal** will need to understand its **place in the herd** in relation to older horses…and these **lessons** begin with its **relationship** with its **mother.**

Once the mare and foal are settled with their herd, the foal can begin to gain strength and learn how things work for a horse. Much of a foal's early life, like any baby's, is spent eating and sleeping. A foal suckles several times an hour and gains 1 to 4 lb (450 g to 1.8 kg) a day. The mother often scratches the top of her foal's rump with her teeth as it suckles, a gesture that evidently comforts and encourages the young one. Many horses can be calmed and settled by gentle scratching in the same place throughout their lives.

Between feeds, the foal will sleep but as soon as it wakes up, it goes straight back for the next feed. The foal will start to play within the first couple of days and spend more time playing, either running and leaping around its mother or with other foals, as it gets stronger day by day. A foal will often gallop in perfect circles around its mother, easily using flying changes—an advanced movement for a ridden horse—to head off in a new direction. It may also buck and rear or leap into the air from all four hooves in high spirits, just like a spring lamb.

As it gets stronger, it can become irritated if its mother wanders off when it wants to feed and may try to stop her by bucking in front of her. While mares are usually very patient, they are quick to administer sharp discipline, usually simply by a swing of the head but sometimes with a nip for a foal that is too pushy. These early encounters are part of the foal's life lessons. It will need to understand its place in the herd in relation to older horses, to learn good manners, and show respect, and these lessons begin with its relationship with its mother.

Growing up

Within a couple of weeks, a new foal will be nibbling at grass and, by around four months old, it will need more nutrition than its mother's milk can provide. By now, its grazing skills will be well established so the foal will simply start to graze alongside her for longer periods of time. Its feed may need supplementing if grazing is poor to support the youngster's rapid growth and development. However, overfeeding can cause growth problems so it's important to choose the correct feeding program for the breed of the foal and the amount and quality of grazing available. A fat foal is no healthier than a fat child; the rapid growth spurts that take place naturally need to be supported, rather than accelerated. Rearing a young horse is no small responsibility and it is not one for a novice owner.

The old saying about not looking a gift horse in the mouth arose because we can tell a horse's age by looking at its teeth. The young foal starts developing milk or baby teeth fairly soon after birth and will have a full set of between 36 and 44 permanent teeth by the age of five. Teething

can be uncomfortable for them and they will chew at wood or stone and dabble with water to ease any discomfort.

Curiosity will also lead the growing foal to try out its new teeth on different grasses, shrubs, and trees. This can lead to trouble, as foals, like babies, tend to explore with their mouths and try chewing anything that they come across. A stray plastic bag can lead to disaster, while hats, coats, and anything left lying around will end up covered with teeth marks. Foals also paw at unfamiliar things with their front feet, fearlessly wandering into the unknown until their mother calls them back to safety. Her sensitivities will teach her foal to be more cautious and, as they grow, foals will also learn from the behavior of the herd. While it may seem strange that they learn to be more wary, rather than less so, a healthy mistrust of anything unfamiliar is essential, so natural curiosity has to be tempered with good sense.

For the first three or four months, the foal will have a soft baby coat and curly whiskers to help it explore and sense the world all around. Then it will shed both and start to show the coat color it will have as an adult. How much this changes over time will depend upon the color, but if it is a solid chestnut or a bay, the chances are that it will change very little. If it is gray, however, it will change throughout its life.

" For the first three or four months, the **foal** will have a **soft baby coat** and curly whiskers… Then it will **shed** both and start to **show** the **coat color** it will have as an **adult**. "

The Lipizzaner is a good example of a breed where there is an extreme color difference between the foal and the adult horse. The dark black or bay foals are as characteristic of the breed as the white-gray mature horses they will become. Appaloosas can also change completely, depending on the coat pattern with which they are born—this alteration can start in the first few months and continue throughout their lives.

The foal will always have whiskers, though the soft baby ones will be replaced by wiry long hairs. Some owners trim the whiskers to create a neater facial outline for showing. However, this is controversial, as an adult horse needs its whiskers as touch sensors as much as a foal does.

As it gets older and bolder, the foal will interact more with other horses, most of whom are very tolerant of youngsters until they are a couple of years old. By that time, they are expected to understand the way the herd works and to recognize appropriate boundaries and good manners. While they are small, older horses will not usually be rough with them, but flattened ears or a swinging neck are warning signs to which they will soon learn to pay attention. If a foal feels threatened or shy, it will reach up to an older horse with a mouthing movement, as though chewing. This is a gesture of appeasement, indicating vulnerability; some horses may also use it in times of stress as adults.

As the foal grows stronger, it will start to venture farther from its mother but will return to her at high speed any time it feels afraid. If she runs, it will keep pace with her, usually leaning into her shoulder for security. This is something young horses continue to do when they are in the early stages of training and some handlers see this as an attempt by the horse to dominate the handler. However, it is more likely to indicate a need for support. By encouraging the young horse not to lean, which is potentially dangerous, the handler may also encourage greater independence.

As the foal takes in more grass, hay, or bucket feeds, it will take in less milk until it no longer needs its mother for nutrition. Traditionally, foals were removed from their mother for weaning at six months old, an often traumatic experience that upset the mare and her foal. In the wild, the foal will show less interest in suckling (and the mother will start to discourage it) over a period of up to a year, or even longer. If the mare is pregnant again, she is more likely to actively sever the connection with the previous foal and some mares can become quite aggressive as their pregnancy progresses. However, others may let the older foal stay close even after the new one is born. Over time, the dependence will lessen. However it happens, this is the natural process and horse owners today are more likely to be sympathetic to it and allow

"In the **wild**, the **foal** will show less interest in **suckling**…over a period of up to a **year**, or even longer. Over time, the **dependence will lessen.**"

Opposite: *Foals develop their confidence and their agility as they run, playfight and chase one another around. But they are quick to return to their mothers if anything takes them by surprise.*

weaning to take place over an extended period of time. One method is to separate the pair for a few minutes at first and then for a few hours, perhaps starting to ride the mother again while leaving the foal at home with companions. This is much easier, and so long as the foal has company, over time it will simply need its mother less and stop suckling.

Older "nanny" mares, or even geldings, can be a great help at this time, giving the foal the comforting presence of an older horse while it develops independence from its mother. Babysitter horses tend to be self-appointed and it's not possible to persuade a horse to keep a foal company if it doesn't have the patience. But in a relaxed herd that know one another well, the foal will be accepted into the group as it grows up, so the weaning and babysitting process will happen naturally.

Colts and fillies

The young horse is called a "foal" until it reaches its first birthday, when it will be known as a "yearling." It may also be described as a "weanling" in the early stages after weaning. A young female horse is known as a "filly," while a young male is a "colt," and they become a "mare" or a "stallion" as they reach breeding maturity, at around three or four depending on their breed and location. Such terms are used differently in different parts of the world. Western trainers tend to refer to young horses coming into training as colts, regardless of gender, while among English Thoroughbred breeders, colts and fillies are young horses under the age of five.

Behavioral differences between colts and fillies become noticeable during their first year. Typically, colts are more likely to playfight, striking with their front feet and biting at the necks of their companions—early signs of stallion behavior. They may also be bolder in their overall attitude. Fillies are more likely to kick out backward but are less inclined to fight. They may be more thoughtful and quicker to learn. However, the personal character of each horse is developing at the same time and individual temperament will outweigh the general pattern—it is not at all unusual to encounter a thoughtful colt and a bold filly.

While a young horse may be physically able to breed at one or two years old, this is generally considered to put too much of a strain on young growing bodies to be good practice. Of course, in the wild horses will breed as soon as their instincts prompt them to or the opportunity arises, which may not be until they are much older, depending on numbers and the availability of mates. Once colts start to show interest in mating, the herd stallion will drive them out to live on the edges of the herd or to leave it completely to join what are known as "bachelor groups." These travel around together until the chance to start their own herd arises.

If there is already a clear leader, he will probably leave to start his own herd with the first available females that the group comes across. Otherwise, fights will arise, which can be very fierce.

A domestic colt is likely to be gelded before he develops stallion behavior and while he's still young enough for it to be a minor operation. Gelding not only makes a male horse easier to handle, it also reduces the number of unwanted foals. As every horse can live for well over 20 years and needs food, training and a secure home all its life, it is essential to manage horse breeding responsibly. A horse kept as a stallion needs to have the characteristics, conformation, and temperament to produce desirable offspring for which it will be easy to find homes. He also needs a handler who understands the challenges, not only of keeping a stallion, but also of handling mares around him when they are in season, as they can prove a handful too. Domestic stallions are often required to live isolated lives to prevent unwanted foals, to stop them fighting with other horses or to avoid the danger of them escaping and pursuing a rider on a mare down the road. Few of them enjoy the relaxed life of a herd living outside with some degree of freedom.

While unrestricted breeding may sound more natural, in the wild many young horses will die or live hard lives at the periphery of a herd. To make sure that doesn't happen in a domestic situation, we have to be realistic—gelding a horse means he can live happily as a herd member with mares and other geldings.

Learning lessons

As the young horse starts to become a full member of the herd, its place within the social order will change. Behavior that is tolerated in a foal or yearling will not be acceptable in a two- or three-year-old. Horses usually warn one another if a boundary has been crossed, but once a youngster stops being a foal and becomes a young horse—a point that other horses will determine in different ways from a human—it will be told off quickly and sharply, usually by means of a lunge or bite, if it doesn't show appropriate respect for its elders. This happens irrespective of size: a small pony will easily remind a much bigger youngster that there are rules of behavior that must be observed. In time, relative position in the herd order will depend largely on the individual character and confidence of the particular horse. Youngsters keep out of the way if there are tussles within the herd and may quickly display the appeasing "mouthing" behavior of a foal if they feel threatened.

The young horse soon learns which of its companions will let it share their food or rub against them and which expect it to keep a distance. Mutual grooming, where two horses stand nose to tail to

In time, relative **position** in the **herd order** will depend largely on the **individual character** and **confidence** of the particular horse.

Opposite: *Friendships between young horses can be very strong and last a lifetime. Even if they are separated for a long period of time, they will recognize one another when they are eventually reunited.*

scratch one another, is a good measure of the level of familiarity. While young horses will usually wait for an older horse to initiate this behavior, the companions they mutually groom will be the ones with which they feel most at ease. These may be mentor figures: much older and stronger characters with an established lead role in the herd to which the young horse becomes attached.

They will also form their own sub-groups with other young horses. These are normally more relaxed and there is more tolerance if the normal boundaries of respect are crossed. However, it's not unusual for a domestic foal to be the only young horse in a small herd. With companions of the same age, the youngster will play and build relationships on two levels; if it is the only youngster, it may still be lucky and find some companions willing to play. Young horses like to run, especially in the early evening, and this is very good for their development. Galloping stretches out the muscles, builds bone density, and matures tissue, as well as helping them become sure-footed.

Part of the argument for the early riding and training of racehorses relates to the benefits it bestows on bone and tissue structure in later life. Racehorses are traditionally started under-saddle as "long yearlings," meaning they are around 18 months old. They will then be raced as two- and three-year-olds, depending on the rules of the competitions administered by different racing bodies. But there are also persuasive arguments that counsel against this level of high-impact work and suggest that a young horse should simply build its strength through plenty of play.

The right age to begin training a young horse is hugely controversial. While different breeds are often held to mature at different rates, few experts would consider any horse to be an adult before it is five years old. Yet backing horses to ride at two, three, and four years is routine, depending on breeding and tradition. Bone formation and other important physical developments play a part in such decisions. Also, and just as importantly, the emotional and mental maturity of a horse will determine if it is ready for work. But before serious work begins, a sensible owner will do some basic training so that the young horse can be haltered, led, and accept simple handling, like grooming and hoof care. This may extend to loading in a trailer, going for walks with an older horse, and showing in-hand. Activities such as horse agility, which teaches a horse to negotiate obstacles confidently while responding to cues from a handler on the ground, also offer opportunities for a young horse to exercise its mind and body.

It is a good idea to introduce short lessons over several days and then perhaps to allow a few weeks to elapse while the horses are just left to play, or

handled as part of the established routine of a herd. Low-pressure ways to introduce a young horse to good manners and interaction with humans include being brought into a barn for regular feeding, being caught to move from one field to another, or standing quietly in turn for hoof trimming.

As two-year-olds, they may tend to throw tantrums, so this can be a good time to build on what they already know about walking quietly or having their feet handled, rather than introducing a lot of new experiences. But when new experiences are introduced in an easy-going way by a confident handler, they will always be accepted more readily.

Quiet insistence on good manners will also reap rewards later on. Teaching a horse to go backward when asked confers a psychological advantage—it not only calms the horse but also establishes that the handler has authority. Expecting a young horse to respect this command is not about domination, but about showing the confident leadership that will reassure the horse. Tantrums and resistance may be signs of character but they are also signs of unease. A horse that learns to respond quietly and promptly to its handler will be more settled and more confident in the long run.

Introducing a young horse to the world and to quiet, relaxed behavior in this way means that when it is time to train it for riding, progress will be much smoother. So while it is vital to let the young horse have plenty of playtime, it also helps to pave the way for later life as a riding or working horse.

Growing up fast

Irrespective of breed, foals tend to follow the same basic growing-up pattern. They are born leggy— even a tiny Miniature Shetland foal, which may be smaller than a dog, will have long legs in relation to its body. This is because they need to be able to stand, run, and feed from birth; foals are born with some advanced physical capabilities that are necessary for their survival.

Foals have small heads and bodies which grow rapidly, but their long legs do not have to grow as fast or as much to reach their adult size. By the time they are around three or four, they will be close to their full height, but they will continue to mature in the body until they are five, or even older in some breeds. This means that their necks will develop and body muscles get rounder or fill out as they grow into their adult form. Many young horses go through phases of being gawky, angular, awkward-looking, perhaps with heads that seem too big. They may also go through a phase of being "croup-high." This means that the rump is higher than the withers; it can be an anxious time for the breeder as a "downhill ride" is not very comfortable and can lead to back problems for horse and rider. However, most croup-high youngsters keep

Left: *Running is part of the fun of being young. It will help to develop muscles and bones, as well as sure-footedness and agility while the youngsters simply enjoy their youthful high spirits.*

growing until their front end catches up with the hindquarters and they level out. By four, the shape of the mature horse is fairly well established and at five, even if there is filling out and growing still to do, the horse is described as an adult.

Particular physical characteristics will show up very early in some breeds. Other traits, such as jumping ability or stamina, may have high potential due to breeding but will be hard to assess until a foal reaches maturity.

Early influences

Young horses grow very quickly and the cute tiny foal phase lasts for only a few months. However, gangly yearlings careering around a field or shy/bold two-year-olds equally ready for a game or a tantrum are just as appealing. Their breed characteristics will determine their color, build, and their overall temperament. But the way they develop as three- and four-year-olds on their journey to adulthood will be largely down to the food, handling, and herd interaction that they experience in the early days. Each foal is an individual influenced by all of these elements, and the horse it grows into will be an individual too. That is both the joy and the challenge of each one.

Each foal is an **individual**…and the horse it grows into will be an individual too. That is both the **joy** and the **challenge** of each one.

Conclusion
The spirit of the horse

Horses are creatures of almost infinite variety. Their physical presence ranges from impressively majestic to the undeniably cute. They can be both fiery thundering creatures with a spirit that is beyond our full comprehension and loving members of the family that we trust implicitly. They impress us, work for us, follow us, become our friends, and even sometimes frighten us. In this book we have glimpsed some of the reasons for the powerful connection that humans have forged with horses over thousands of years.

As herd animals, horses are trainable and cooperative, responsive to confident leadership. This complements their need as prey animals to seek places and situations where they feel at ease and not in imminent danger. Their strong grace and instinctive senses enable us to ride them in genuine partnership, while the subtlety of their spirit has woven them a special place in myth and legend. All of these elements, combined with their natural variety of shape, size, color, and temperament, make the horse a wonderfully appealing companion for both work and leisure.

However, the closer we look, the more we realize that this relationship is a responsibility for us as their handlers and riders. Horses are not resources designed for our benefit—they are living creatures with individual characters, strong instincts, and their own needs and motivations for safety and survival. Thousands of years ago, when humans started to domesticate them, we altered their future forever. But they changed us too and this complex partnership has shaped human culture.

If we take on the leadership role with sensitivity, we can begin to benefit from understanding the horse's approach to life. We can learn about group dynamics by watching them; we can learn about relaxation and energy too. Humans are hunters, more akin to pack animals than herd animals, yet we share many common features, especially the need to be part of a social group and to know our place in the network of relationships that develops around us. Horses appeal to us because we are both like them and profoundly unlike them. The equine trust in instinct, the love of movement, and the enjoyment of simply hanging out with companions can teach us a great deal. Horses can help humans find a way to balance our driven modern lifestyles with a more relaxed approach. They are happier around quiet, confident people. We are happier people if we are quiet and confident. This win-win situation becomes possible as soon as we start interacting with horses.

Outside my window, the summer is quickly moving into fall. The moors have turned from purple to brown and scarlet berries hang like early

Christmas decorations on the mountain ash trees. My horses are starting to wander down to the barn in the mornings, hoping for breakfast, and their glossy summer coats are thickening in readiness for winter. I'll try to leave their rugs off for as long as possible so that they grow good coats and acclimatize to the colder weather.

Each member of my herd has slightly different needs. Darius is an old man now so I'll add a supplement to his feed for his stiff shoulders. Topaz is a rescue horse and gets anxious if he can't easily get outside, so I always make sure his food is in the open front of the barn. Rowan is half Welsh Cob and what's known as a "good doer" so I have to watch her weight. The two donkeys don't like rain so they tend to hang around inside in bad weather cadging extra hay.

Baby Ruby isn't really a baby anymore and she's grown well over the summer. She's filled out too and there are glimpses of the horse she'll grow into, not very tall but sturdy like her Quarter Horse mother and elegant like her Appaloosa father. She's a chocolate *grulla* like her mother, but there are a few white hairs on her hip—this is the Appaloosa roaning that may develop as she gets older. She's still getting used to the wild Welsh winters and I want her to put her energy into growing, not keeping warm, so she'll have a rug on soon. It will be a month later than last year though, when she was newly arrived. The Miniature Shetlands will be going home soon but they'll be back next spring when the grass starts to grow. The two herds know each other so well now that I can tell that they will pick up just where they left off this year.

Horses bring rhythm into our lives. They live by the patterns of their instinct, their herd, and the seasons. By watching and caring for them, we can develop our sensitivities to the world around us—learning to read the signs of rain, snow, high winds, hot sun, spring grass, and winter mud. We appreciate body language when dealing with animals that use it as their main form of communication. We can experience the thrill of four-legged movement and a sensation of speed that are unknown in our bipedal way of life. The enjoyment of their beauty, grace, and physical presence is only the starting point for all that a love of horses has to offer us.

I hope that you have found photographs and ideas in this book to help you connect with the rhythm of the horse, and to understand a bit more about its needs and subtleties of character. For every floating mane and majestic head, there are also shaggy thatches and round cuddly bodies. They are all beautiful, all full of character, and all ready to make friends with humans—a deep instinct that is our great good fortune.

Glossary

barefoot a hoof-care approach that mimics natural wear in the wild to make the hooves stronger, thus eliminating the need for shoes.

bit a means of communication with the horse using a metal, rubber, or plastic bar in the mouth to which the reins are attached.

breed a strain of horse having specific characteristics—usually developed by deliberate selection for those features.

breed standard a list of defining characteristics accepted by a breed society.

classical riding also known as classical dressage or *haute école* (high school), a style of riding based on the natural movement of stallions developed into a series of athletic, dancelike movements; this is the foundation of modern dressage.

cob a small stocky horse or pony, known as a type with a steady nature.

colt a young male horse.

dilution a gene that causes a horse's coat color to become lighter in appearance.

endurance riding a competitive sport over long distances and often challenging terrain, where the fitness and speed of the horse are taken into account.

feral an animal from domesticated stock that has returned to a wild state.

filly a young female horse.

flying change when the horse changes direction at canter without breaking pace to a trot.

forage a feeding regime based on dried natural grasses.

gene a segment of DNA that provides a blueprint of genetic information. Genes hold the information to build and maintain an organism's cells and pass genetic traits to offspring.

hand the traditional unit of measurement of a horse's height, so-called because it is based on the width of a man's hand. One hand measures 4 in (10.16 cm). The abbreviation "hh" means "hands high."

herd an interdependent group of horses, either in the wild or in a domestic setting. To the horse, any number greater than one is a herd and this group may include regular handlers or even other animals.

heterozygous a pair of genes that are different.

homozygous a pair of genes that are the same.

imprinting the instinctive learning process of a newborn animal that operates through recognition and bonding to its mother or a mother substitute, not necessarily of its own kind.

modifier a gene that influences the physical appearance of a horse.

mutual grooming when horses groom one another, an act of trust and bonding as well as a practicality.

points the mane, tail, legs, and tips of the ears of a horse.

recessive a gene with characteristics that will be hidden when a dominant gene has control.

Index

Picture credits

© Shutterstock.com: Volodymyr Burdiak 58-59, 205; Acon Cheng 29; constantine 202-203; DavidYoung 188-189; eastern light photography 50; Iakov Filimonov 98-99; Francey 126-127; Greenfire 178-179; gurinaleksandr 52-53; J. Helgason 16-17; Nicole Hollenstein 78; alersandr hunta 34-35; Olga_i 36-37, 44-45, 124-125, 128-129, 148-149, 150-151, 168-169; jacotakepics 118-119; Gail Johnson 49; Alexia Khruscheva 4-5, 104-105, 108-109; kislovas 12-13; Abramova Kseniya 114-115; Andrzej Kubik 130-131; Eduard Kyslynskyy 94, 186, 208-209, 214-215; lebanmax 96-97; Lenkadan 138-139, 172-173, 174-175, 190-191, 192-193; Neil Lockhart 20-21, 220-221; mariait 42, 102-103, 112; Miramiska 26-27; Kachalkin Oleg 30-31; Regien Paassen 40-41; pirita 116, 142-143, 176-177; Jeanne Provost 32, 39, 46-47; Scott E Read 8-9; Julia Remezova 182-183; Dmitry Saparov 216-217; smeola 68-69, 185; E. Spek 156-157; Michael Steden 120-121; TDway 196-197; Makarova Viktoria 2-3, 54-55, 66-67, 90-91, 123, 134-135; Zuzule 137, 140-141, 152, 162-163, 166, 167, 171, 194, 198-199, 206, 211.

© Getty Images: John Cancalosi 158; Maria itina 180-181; Frank Lukasseck 22-23; Laura Palazzolo 164-165; Jaana-Marja Rotinen 160-161; Marcus Rudolph 154-155; Anett Somogyvari 62, 146-147; Christiana Stawski 14.

© Wojciech Kwiatkowski: 1, 11, 18-19, 24-25, 57, 61, 64-65, 70-71, 72-73, 74-75, 76, 80-81, 82, 84-85, 86-87, 88-89, 93, 100, 106-107, 132-133, 144, 200, 212.

© Steve Rawlins: 111.